Cowgirl Poetry

other Western books from Gibbs Smith, Publisher:

Art of the Boot
Tyler Beard, photographs by Jim Arndt

Cowboy Chic: Western Style Comes Home
Chase Reynolds Ewald

Cowboy Curmudgeon and Other Poems
Wallace McRae, illustrations by Clinton McRae

Cowboy Poetry: A Gathering
edited and with an introduction by Hal Cannon

Humorous Cowboy Poetry: A Knee-Slappin' Gathering

Last Buckaroo (a novel)
Mackey Hedges

New Cowboy Poetry: A Contemporary Gathering
edited and with an introduction by Hal Cannon

Salsas
Susan Curtis and Kathi Long

Singing Cowboy Stars
Robert W. Phillips

Sweet Treats from the Wild West
Chase Reynolds Ewald and Amy Jo Sheppard

**The Santa Fe School of Cooking Cookbook:
Spirited Southwestern Recipes**
Susan Curtis

Tacos
Susan Curtis and Daniel Hoyer, with R. Allen Smith

**Where the Wind Lives:
A Sister's Song from the Homestead**
Linda Hussa

Wild, Wild West Cowboy Cookies
Tuda Libby Crews

COWGIRL POETRY

ONE HUNDRED YEARS
OF
RIDIN' & RHYMIN'

edited & with an introduction
by Virginia Bennett

GIBBS·SMITH
→P
PUBLISHER

SALT LAKE CITY

*To that daring cowgirl, imagined or otherwise,
in every woman.*

First Edition
05 04 03 02 01   5 4 3 2 1

Text copyright © 2001 by Virginia Bennett
Each poet retains copyright to her poem(s)
Illustrations copyright © 2001 by Meghan Merker

Published by
Gibbs Smith, Publisher
P.O. Box 667
Layton, Utah 84041

Orders: (1-800) 748-5439
www.gibbs-smith.com

Designed and produced by Meghan Merker
Front cover illustration originated from a pre-1920s movie poster
Border illustrations by Meghan Merker

Printed and bound in the United States of America

Library of Congress Cataloging-in-Publication Data

Cowgirl poetry: 100 years of ridin' and rhymin'/edited and with an
introduction by Virginia Bennett.—1st ed.
  p. cm.
  ISBN 1-58685-016-4
1. Cowgirls—Poetry. 2. American poetry—Women authors.
3. American poetry—20th century. 4. Women—West (U.S.)—Poetry. 5.
American poetry—West (U.S.) 6. West (U.S.)—Poetry. 7. Ranch life—Poetry
I. Bennett, Virginia, 1952
Feb. 18 –

PS595.C6 C75 2001
811'.5080636—dc21
                                        00-045677

CONTENTS

Introduction   ix
Acknowledgments   xiii

THOSE WHO'VE GONE BEFORE

The Range Call - *Rhoda Sivell*   15
The Ranch in the Coulee - *Gwendolyn Haste*   16
Herd a-Passin' - *Dee Strickland Johnson*   17
Grass - *Maggie Mae Sharp*   19
Hail and Farewell - *Delia Gist Gardner*   21
All That Is Left - *Virginia Bennett*   23
Roses for a Cowgirl - *Jo Maseburg*   24
The Edge - *Debra Coppinger Hill*   27
Little Jo Monaghan - *A. Kathy Moss*   29
Brander Sisters - *June Brander Gilman*   31
Lilac Time - *Gwen Petersen*   33
Heaven's Branding - *Janet Parkhurst*   37

GROWING UP WESTERN

Jinglin' the Horses Home - *Janet Moore*   41
Rain in the Night - *Myrt Wallis*   43
Wild Morning Glories - *Sharlot Hall*   44
His Cowgirl Rides the Copper Horse
   - *Linda Hussa*   45
I Never Wanted to "Mother Up" - *Sally Bates*   46
The Hired Man - *Jody Strand*   48
Be Yourself - *Georgie Sicking*   50
The Overseer - *Lyn DeNaeyer*   52
The Cowtank - *Barbara Bockelman*   55
Independence - *Pat Frolander*   57
Hot Iron - *Deanna Dickinson McCall*   58

A COWGIRL & HER HORSE

Fredonia - *Dee Strickland Johnson* 60
She Loved Her Horses - *Elizabeth Ebert* 62
For Brandy at Age 21 - *Laurie Wagner Buyer* 65
Ridin' - *Linda Bark'karie* 66
The Muster - *Australie* 67
El Fuego de Sonora - *Virginia Bennett* 68
An Owner's Lament - *Veronica Weal* 70
Little Horse - *Myrt Wallis* 73
To Foxy - *Kay Kelley* 74
The Greatest Sport - *Georgie Sicking* 76
Country Girls - *Marion Fitzgerald* 78
Listen - *Debra Coppinger Hill* 79

A COWGIRL & HER WORK

Post Script: Texas Wimmen - *Helen B. Odom* 81
Where the Pelican Builds - *Mary Hannay Foote* 82
A Little Red Self-Propelled Baler - *Lisa Quinlan* 83
Round-Up Hand - *Carole Jarvis* 86
His Place or Mine - *Audrey Hankins* 89
Generic Titles - *Sally Bates* 91
Cowgirls of the '30s - *June Brander Gilman* 92
Dry Camps - *Sally Bates* 95
The Bay with the Star and a Snip - *Veronica Weal* 96
Shouldn't We Go to the House for a Horse?
   - *Echo Roy* 99
The Cook - *Myrt Wallis* 102
Hands of Leather - *Maggie Mae Sharp* 105

LIVING WITH NATURE & ANIMALS

Cattle - *Berta Hart Nance*   108
Mother to Mother - *Charlotte Thompson*   109
The Rhyme of the Pronghorns - *Mary Austin*   110
Coyote Song - *LindaM. Hasselstrom*   112
Among Udder Things - *Marion Fitzgerald*   115
Somethin' Strange - *Jo Casteel*   118
The Granny Cow - *Audrey Hankins*   119
Four-Leaf Clover - *Katie Kidwell*   120
The Lone Post - *Dele Ball*   121
Stinky Tenant - *Terry Henderson*   123
Lone Dog - *Irene Rutherford McLeod*   124
Hank Warner's Lucky Burro - *Peggy Godfrey*   125
Sammy Blue's Rabbit Chasing Days
   - *Laurie Wagner Buyer*   127
Smell of Rain - *Sharlot Hall*   128
Another Drought - *B. Lynne McCarthy*   130

THE HEART OF A COWGIRL

The Bucking Bronco - *Unknown*   133
Our Last Ride - *Rhoda Sivell*   134
For Fred - *Kay Shean*   135
Yellow Slicker - *Debra Coppinger Hill*   136
Return - *Linda Hussa*   138
Unfaithful - *Jody Strand*   139
Skipping Rocks - *Marie W. Smith*   141
The Hired Man's Wife - *Jody Strand*   142
Tomboy - *Dee Strickland Johnson*   144
Horseback, Through Snow
   - *Laurie Wagner Buyer*   146
You Ride Away - *Evelyn Mellard*   147
Cowboy Courtin' Time - *Elizabeth Ebert*   148
Little Duck - *Carol Oxley*   150

LOVE OF THE LAND & THE LIFESTYLE

They Keep a-Stealing on You in the Night
  - *Rhoda Sivell 153*
The Cattleman's Prayer - *Jo Becksted 154*
Ridin' - *Deanna Dickinson McCall 156*
The Darkest Hour - *Carmel Randle 157*
Livin' Free - *Rhonda Sedgwick Stearns 162*
The First Sure Signs of Spring - *Carole Jarvis 164*
An Old Monarch - *Barney Nelson 166*
Real Wealth - *Peggy Godfrey 167*
Sure Am Lucky - *Jo Casteel 169*
100 Years from Now - *Doris Daley 170*
The Silence - *Jo Casteel 173*
Wrong Road - *Audrey Hankins 174*

OBSERVATIONS ON LIFE & MEN

Man-sized Job - *Sharlot Hall 176*
Two Dogs - *Deb Carpenter 177*
Hats Off - *Charlotte Thompson 178*
Mortgage One Good Wife - *Yvonne Hollenbeck 179*
Vera - *Carmel Randle 182*
A Blinding Hell of Driving Snow - *Kit McLean 184*
July Thunderstorms - *June Brander Gilman 185*
Geezers and Crones - *Gwen Petersen 187*
Keeping an Eye Out - *Linda M. Hasselstrom 189*
Bones - *Doris Daley 191*

INTRODUCTION

She is the woman every little girl dreamed of becoming, capable yet cloyingly helpless, spunky yet charming. She was Calamity Jane or Annie Oakley of the silver screen. She was the classy heroine once romanticized in the blue glow of an old, black-and-white Zenith television set, and she rode a high-steppin' buckskin horse beside her handsome husband, Roy, trotting toward the camera and singing "Happy Trails To You" with a dazzling smile and a friendly wave.

Somewhere tonight, there is another woman sitting down to a desk, spilling words onto a page of blank paper. She may be on a ranch owned by her family or perhaps she is part of a husband/wife team working for wages at a large outfit owned by a faceless corporation. Her house may be a little employee's quarters or a log palace rivaling *Bonanza*'s Ponderosa. She may be carrying on a multigenerational tradition, or she might be the first in her family to work on a western ranch with horses and cattle. Yet, there are common denominators that indelibly bind together all of these inspired, and inspiring, women.

The poet of which I speak has lived with nature and hard work. She has dirt under her fingernails more often than not, and is not averse to doing any chore on the ranch that needs doing, whether it's feeding the crew, cleaning out the hired man's house that has been left trashed by disgruntled employees, or pulling with all of her strength on a pair of OB chains, icy cold and slippery from blood and amniotic fluid, in a desperate attempt to deliver a calf born too big. She takes her kids to school, or home-schools them. She rides the horses available, sometimes even the "broncy" one disdained by the ranch hands. She's moved cows with a child perched on a pillow in the saddle in front of her. She does what must be done.

The cowgirl still exists. And we are blessed that she is willing to write about it. However, the sheer volume of submissions received whenever an anthology of women's writings of the West is being compiled tells us that this woman, penning her thoughts between ranch chores, is a commonplace occurrence. I have worked on guest ranches where visitors have never heard of cowboy/cowgirl poetry. And so, for many of you, *Cowgirl Poetry* is a world waiting to be explored.

Within these pages, the reader will find the beginning of a fresh journey down a trail of honest observances, where there is a commonality shared in all human experience. Though the reader has not personally worked in the sizzling hay-season heat on an admired "Little Red Self-Propelled Baler" (poem by Lisa Quinlan), he or she can relate to hardship, responsibility, honorable work ethic and desire to please one's parents. When we read of the lonely little girl on the porch in Dee Strickland Johnson's "Herd a-Passin'," we envision her waiflike form and travel back to our own "lonesomes," when just a wave from a passerby gave us courage to dream.

Vintage writings were a rich discovery. "Hail and Farewell," found recited as a dramatic ending to Gail Steiger's CD of truthful cowboy music, was penned by

Delia Gist Gardner, whose husband, Gail Gardner, wrote many classic cowboy poems, including "The Sierry Petes," (better known as "Tying Knots in the Devil's Tail"). Steiger related that no one knew that his grandmother had been a writer, yet after her death, this single poem was found among her things.

While organizing a flow for this volume, a classic poem often turned out to be the perfect companion piece to a contemporary one, as in the case of "The Rhyme of the Pronghorns" (Mary Austin, 1920s) and Linda Hasselstrom's "Coyote Song." Such incidents illustrate the ongoing heritage of western women's writing, with hopeful scenarios that a hundred years from now women will still be writing of their experiences and emotions that are similar to that of the cowgirl at the turn of the twentieth century.

What has kept cowgirls writing for the last hundred years? We can only guess that those female authors of decades ago were influenced by the same motivations women enjoy today. Some may write and not feel the need to share with others, but I feel certain that for most cowgirl poets, the moving force to write of their experiences has been acceptance. Her family, friends, neighbors and community have cheered her on and bought her self-published chapbooks, run off on a copy machine in town, saddle-stapled and offered up as one offers one's soul to God: take this, it is all of me, it is who I am, treat me kindly.

Faith plays a large role in the writing of western women. Not only faith in God and Creator, a topic often touched upon in these pages, but faith that the weather will change, the rain will come, your horse won't stumble, but if he does you will survive, and if you don't, all will turn out for the best, for ranch women know too well that nature continues, and we're all just a part of the plan.

Surviving with style demands a healthy sense of humor, and comic relief factors playfully within many a cowgirl's poem. Women can relate to anyone and write in any voice, be it their husband's or father's, or that of the family milk cow, as in Marion Fitzgerald's "Among Udder Things."

This collection spans decades of writings and includes American, Canadian and Australian poets in a broad spectrum of styles. In whatever form they are written, I guarantee that these poems are not only entertaining but authentic, and that they will ring true to the ear of any dyed-in-the-wool cowboy or cowgirl. They are presented here for the enjoyment of readers everywhere who want to experience a little slice of wild and fun-loving cowgirl life. Let's trot down that happy trail Dale Evans wished for us fifty years ago! And don't forget to smile and wave!

—*Virginia Bennett*

ACKNOWLEDGEMENTS

Beyond thanking all the gifted women who submitted their heartfelt poetry for this volume, the editor would like to convey appreciation to those who helped "round up" some of the outstanding classic poetry herein. Barney Nelson of Alpine, Texas, was invaluable in providing several examples of early-twentieth-century cowgirl writing. Carmel Randle of Queensland, Australia, proved a willing resource of not only contemporary women's "bush poetry" but classic work as well, including the oldest poem within this collection. Gwen Peterson of Big Timber, Montana shared her knowledge of Montana women's poetry, and David Stanley of Westminster College, Salt Lake City, shared his findings of work by Sharlot Hall and Rhoda Sivell (whose work found its way to the editor from Stanley via Doris Daley of Calgary, Alberta). When we began this project, we were not sure that, as women, we even had any classic poets to refer back to. Now we know that there is a rich and full history of women who worked with cattle and horses, and who put those experiences on paper for us all to savor. I encourage readers who enjoy the classic work within this anthology to find other work by these poets, all of whom were prolific in their writing.

THOSE
WHO'VE GONE
BEFORE

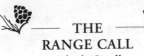

THE RANGE CALL
Rhoda Sivell
1912

I'm lonely to-night for the old range,
  And the voices I loved to hear;
Though the band in the town is playing,
  The music comes soft to my ear.
There's only the river between us,
  The town in the flat shows bright,
But I'm lonely, lonely, lonely,
  For my old range home to-night.

I'm lonely to-night for the old friends;
  For new friends can never be
Just what those dear old range friends
  Have been in the past to me.
But I hear their voices calling,
  And the band has ceased to play,
And my heart has gone out from the gas-lit town
  To the wild range far away.

If ever you hear the range call,
  The voice that speaks soft and sweet;
That wins you back to the prairie,
  Away from the gas-lit street;
If once you hear her calling,
  You sure then have got to go,
For the old range is waiting for you,
  And you've got to love her so.

THE RANCH
IN THE COULEE
Gwendolen Haste
1930

He built a ranch house down a little draw,
So that he should have wood and water near.
The bluffs rose all around. She never saw
The arching sky, the mountains lifting clear;
But to the west the close hills fell away
And she could glimpse a few feet of the road.
The stage to Roundup went by every day,
Sometimes a rancher town-bound with his load,
An auto swirling dusty through the heat,
Or children trudging home on tired feet.

At first she watched it as she did her work,
A horseman pounding by gave her a thrill,
But then within her brain began to lurk
The fear that if she lingered from the sill
Someone might pass unseen. So she began
To keep the highroad always within sight,
And when she found it empty long she ran
And beat upon the pane and cried with fright.
The winter was the worst. When snow would fall
He found it hard to quiet her at all.

From *Montana Margins, A State Anthology,* Joseph Kinsey Howard, ed.
(New Haven, Connecticut: Yale University Press, 1930). Used with permission.

— HERD A-PASSIN' —
Dee Strickland Johnson
Payson, Arizona - 1999

I can see, this early mornin',
In the soft gray light of dawn,
A cloud of dust a-risin'
As a herd comes movin' on.

Now the rosy glow of sunrise
Turns them dust clouds into red,
While the earth, still cool from sleepin',
Rises, stretchin', from her bed,

Like me. Inside the dugout
Ma's a-stirrin' round the room.
Pa, he'll soon be out here cussin'
"Them dang cattle!" passin' soon.

I stand out here every mornin'
Jest to say hello to day,
And to let Pa get his clothes on
And to stay out of the way;

But mostly, I look south and north
Over hot, dry plains of sand
To see if anybody's comin'
'Crost this lonesome level land.

Bud's little yaller head pops out,
All tousled from his sleep;
But his eyes are bright and shinin';
Still, I'd really rather keep

These moments for myself alone
When the herd fills up the space,
And I kinely wave my fingers
As one cowboy spies our place.

Oh! I swear I'd seen him raise his hand
And touch his wide-brimmed hat!
Why, my heart is nigh to bustin'
Just to think on such as that!

I hear Ma callin' *"Sadie!*
You come get yourself inside!"
But I see that cowboy turn and wave!
And before the dust subsides,

I know his eyes are soft and brown
And I know his hair is, too,
Even though this chokin' dust
I couldn't possibly see through!

Well, now I've got a secret
For to carry in my heart
To help me when the lonesomes
Likes to tear my soul apart.

I'll jest think on that slight cowboy
With the herd dust boilin' round.
(How'd I know his face was gentle
And his eyes was warm and brown?)

Inspired by S. Omar Barker's "Grainger's Daughter"

GRASS

Maggie Mae Sharp

1996 National Lady Cowboy Poet

Black Forest, Colorado - 1998

It was a single blade of new, green grass
that now lay gently in her hand—
Its importance not apparent
to those who may not understand . . .

It was a blade of grass, the darkest green
from this northern meadow crest—
And with no bugs, no blight, no sunburned tip,
it was one as perfect as the rest.

So important because . . . it was *his* grass, his
    favorite strain
put down the year he took her hand.
They bought this place, some late in life—
And it had become more work than they had
planned.

But they'd worked together, side by side
for many years before he died—
They'd laughed and loved on better days
and on others, fought and cried.

She recalled the day they'd tilled the soil
up on this northern meadow ground,
And she remembered how he'd shed a tear
as he lay that first seed down.

19

For it was a dream they both had shared,
the dream of ownin' land—
And when two souls can share the same bright dream
there isn't much that can't be had.

She remembered all the foals that grazed
upon this northern meadow land—
And with fondness, all the fine, strong stock
that had come to wear their brand.

A pleasant gust of summer wind,
and the blade of grass, no longer seen—
A thinning wisp of silver hair . . .
now lays blowing gently through the green.

A small leathered hand, now graces green
as if reaching out for his—
An aging heart . . . beats one last time . . .
and on weathered lips, the cold, sweet smile of bliss.

Today, it's still a single blade of new, green grass,
one just as perfect as the rest—
And it thrives as it grows, above them both
up on that northern meadow crest.

HAIL AND FAREWELL

(Reflection from a cabin in Skull Valley, Arizona,
over an old Indian camping ground, about 1945)

Delia Gist Gardner

Think not on my brittle bones mingling with dust, for
These
Are but a handful added
To those gone before.
Think, rather, that on this borrowed hilltop
One lived joyously, and died content.

In this dark soil
I found reminders, saying:
"You, too, will pass; savor for us
The wind and the sun."

From the smoke-blackened earth
I dug
A frail, shell bracelet, shaped lovingly, skillfully,
For a brown-skinned wrist, now dust.
The broken piece of clay
Was a doll's foot and leg, artfully curved,
Made for a brown-eyed child.

Pottery shards saying:
"Yours for a little time only.
Take delight in this, as we did."

The tree will die: the vine wither and rattle in the wind.
For I broke a law of Nature.
I carried water to the hilltop. Nevertheless,
For those after me there will be
These things I have loved:

Morning sun rays, slanting across the hilltop,
Lighting the great trees in the green meadow.
Wind, the great blue sky,
Peace of the encircling hills
And flaming glow of sunset.

ALL THAT IS LEFT

Virginia Bennett
Winthrop, Washington - 1992

At the mouth of a redrock canyon
Near the base of a sandstone cliff
She stands there, a skeleton sentinel
With branches arthritic and stiff.
And those upturned fingers appear to pray
For water, though now, it's too late.
Not far from her roots lies a rusty stove lid,
And the remains of a barbed-wire gate.

Not much, you might think, of a legacy,
Not much to remember them by.
Yet this site speaks readable volumes
To the wise and experienced eye.
And the tree, though now dead, says something,
An echo from a waterless grave.
For it tells of the hope of a homesteader,
And of the sacrifice somebody gave.

She stands enshrined, a personification
Of dreams and desires and grit.
For that old cottonwood was the first thing planted
When the flame of faith was lit.
Thriving under a pan of daily dishwater,
Her leaves a light color of jade,
Barefoot children swung from her branches
And a mother snapped beans in her shade.

But drought sucked the life from the homesteader,
Who eventually had to move on.
And within a few years, the tree also withered
When its daily washwater was gone.
So, today, she stands guard in the canyon,
And each storm brings a new limb to the ground,
And every spring, during the desert roundup,
Weary cowboys delight in the kindling they've found.

ROSES FOR A COWGIRL
Jo Maseberg
Macksville, Kansas - 2000

"Don't bring me roses till I die,"
She told him all her life.
"I'm more a lilac kind of girl,
A daisy kind of wife."

"I just can't stand to see them cut,"
She finally confessed.
"It's hard to raise a rose out here—
The soil just ain't the best."

But she had tried so many years.
Had tried, and failed each time.
The sun too hot, the nights too cold . . .
It seemed to him a crime

The way the country fought her blooms.
And how she loved that land
Despite its spiteful ways and means,
Its hellish sun and sand.

"You haven't got me licked!" she'd yell
As hail would pelt her buds.
And then she'd smile a little bit,
As though to recant her words.

"It likes to play," she told him once.
"It's like a game, you see.
I want to have my roses but
The country wants me free."

She always had seemed free to him,
Especially on her horse.
She rode as wildly as the wind
Her own unchallenged course.

And she would smile at anything,
From blizzards raging mean
To baby fawns and their first steps
In meadows rolling green.

They never had a babe to love,
She gave her life to him.
She cowgirled almost sixty years,
Until her eyes grew dim.

But today he bought her roses,
The time had fin'lly come.
For two long years he'd left her lay,
Unable to return.

He walked the trail in old, worn boots,
The roses in his arms,
Till, finally topping out the hill
He saw the mounds and stones.

And there, a ways away from all,
A-lookin' to the west,
Her stone stood, waiting still
While she took one last rest.

He took the last few steps with tears
Behind his weary eyes.
He'd thought he'd seen it all before,
But there was one surprise.

For there her roses bloomed bright red,
Their stems still in the ground.
The country finally let her win,
He thought as tears came down,

They bowed their heads at him as if
To chide him for being late.

"Well darlin', I know your roses
Were worth the long, hard wait."

THE EDGE
Debra Coppinger Hill
Chelsea, Oklahoma - 1998

"It will be a Long-day,"
You would say, as you checked the cinch.
And with that, I would know
Not to expect you
Until darkness had begun.

Into the tall grass
You would ride.
And I, left here,
Set the cabin straight
And fed and watered and gathered eggs.

On the Long-days
We lived in two worlds:
Yours, an open prairie covered in cattle.
Mine, a homestead covered in dust.

I often wondered
If that same wind that so tormented me
Was the same wind
That you spoke of as magical.

I did not love this world then;
I only loved you.
And it was you,
And you alone,
Who made it bearable.

On the Long-days,
Knowing you would come back
Tired yet satisfied and pleased,
I wrote the letters to the family
And lied about the love
I had for this place.

Then, you did not ride in.
They found the broken shell of you,
The horse dead too,
Where you had shot it to save its suffering,
Never mind that you suffered also.
Family and friends tell me
That this place is too much for me alone.
But I cannot . . . and . . . will not
leave.

This place owes me your spirit.
And I will wait here
Until it comes in the wind
And pushes the dust away.
Until it picks me up
And dances me across the prairie
And into your arms

At the edge of the darkness
Where you ride

At the end
Of a Long-day.

— LITTLE JO MONAGHAN —
A. Kathy Moss
Canyon City, Oregon - 1999

Little Jo Monaghan, a legend in his time,
Traveled to Ruby, Idaho, with gold on his mind.
Back in 1868, he rode in with all he had,
At scarcely five foot tall, he was a fragile-looking lad.
He never saw inside a bunkhouse, he preferred out
   under the stars,
He never cussed or smoked, and always stayed away
   from bars.
He rode broncs a different way with a gentle sort
   of hand,
"Cowboy Jo" soon he was named across the western
   land.
He moved into Oregon and built a shack out on
   his spread.
Bought some cattle and with that, a quiet life he led.
For twenty years, he made some friends but alone he
   always stayed.
A mystery to some, a legend to others, what he was
   dealt he played.
One day in 1903, a friend stopped by Jo's home
To find him deathly ill, Jo would never more roam.
They gathered in the streets to hear of Little Jo's
   death.
But what was found out after he had taken his
   last breath
Was that Jo was actually Josephine,
   a woman in disguise.

She had lived a life as a man all these years, to the
    town's surprise,
To feed a child that she had bore, in others' eyes a
    disgrace,
From New York, she moved out west, she never saw
    his face.
And she may have lived alone, and forever may
    she rest,
For she died a proud woman, in a man's world done
    her best.

BRANDER SISTERS
June Brander Gilman
Drummond, Montana

Those sisters of mine were cowgirls fine
Who asked no favors and wanted no pity,
As they put on a show at any rodeo
From Calgary to New York City.
High spirited, honest, and moralistic,
They travelled the circuit alone;
They didn't follow the trail hitched to anyone's tail,
But made it all on their own.

They would trust to luck with horses that buck
And draw their mounts from the hat with the men,
Then raise their eyes to the Lord in the skies
And pray they'd be back tomorrow to try again.
They were the only two gals I've ever heard of
Who rode double on the wild Brahma steer,
One on the neck and the other on back,
As the audience would loudly cheer.

They owned their own string of fast horses,
Which they would enter in the relay race,
Where riders changed horses on each half-mile lap,
And more than once they came in, in first place.
They would enter the wild-cow milking contest,
Always as a two-girl team,
To rope and hold the mean, ornery critter
And into a pop bottle milk a stream.

The Roman-riding race was a daring feat,
With two racehorses tied at the cinch,
A pad on the back and rider erect
With nothing but the toes to clinch.
There were few who cared or even dared
To try this balancing act,
Standing a-top two steeds while going full speed
Around the half-mile track.
Though several teams would enter the race,
With each rider for victory a-thirst,
On the final stretch ahead by a neck,
'Twas my sister who came in first.

In between the rodeo seasons
You could find them riding the range,
And when things got slow, they gave their own rodeo
To garner a little extra change.
Yes, these sisters of mine were cowgirls fine,
And though they acquired not fortune or fame,
I'm proud to recall how they gave it their all
As they lived and played the game!

LILAC TIME

Gwen Petersen
Big Timber, Montana - 1995

On a windswept prairie sparsely set
With tiny homestead shacks,
A man and a woman partnered there
In work that bent their backs.

Their rough-built home was chinked with sod
And planted round with trees;
A lilac bush grew near the door,
Spring blooms for honeybees.

They scraped and saved to prove up land;
In places, soil was thin,
But water flowed and bunchgrass grew,
And wild hay teased by wind.

Here they chose to settle down,
And here they chose to stay;
Life was good; they hoped for a child
Come lilac time in May.

They stocked black Angus, good beef cows,
Cash crop of white-faced ewes.
A flock of hens, a soft-eyed Jersey,
Even a pig or two.

Each morning they turned the sheep to graze
Among the grassy swales;
At dusk on Blaze, she brought them home
Ahead of coyotes' wails.

And spring brought calf and lambing time,
By turns they checked the stock
For newborn calves and fresh-dropped lambs,
All night around the clock.

As weather warmed and days grew long
In summer on the ranch,
She'd saddle Blaze, he'd ride Big Red
To every schoolhouse dance.

Their son was born that second spring
When lilacs burst with beauty.
She sewed him clothes; from homespun yarn
She knitted tiny booties.

A lively child with sunny smiles,
She took him everywhere;
She put a pillow on her saddle,
And let him cowboy there.

The boy grew strong all summer long
And as the fall progressed,
His laughter filled their home with joy,
They knew that they were blessed.

Then winter came; the boy took sick,
She doctored him and prayed.
He seemed to rally, then grew weak,
His life began to fade.

"I got to take the boy to town,
His breathing's awful bad."
But how to travel the wintry road?
A horse was all they had.

"It's pitch dark now, the snow's too deep."
He said, his face so drawn and grim,
"Can't go nowheres until it's light;
The trail is drifted in."

All night she packed the baby's chest
With poultices and balm;
She listened to his rasping breath,
And made herself stay calm.

At dawn's first light, she told her man,
"Can't get his fever down;
You got to stay and feed the stock,
I'll take the boy to town."

She saddled Blaze out in the barn,
And cried into his mane,
"We got to get the boy to town."
Blaze got extra grain.

Hooves crunched snow. He watched her come.
She struggled round a drift.
He clasped their child in gentle hands,
As if he held a gift.

His throat constricted, voice wire-tight,
His words scratched rough as gravel,
"Our boy—he died there in my arms;
Old Blaze—don't need to travel."

They fenced the grave near the lilac bush
And asked their God to bless;
And on a marker carved these words,
"Here lies our baby, Jess."

The homestead's gone, nothing remains
Except the lilac brave,
And a few gray boards of a picket fence
Built round a tiny grave.

Out here in the West, where settlers dwelt
On plains as vast as a sea,
Lie the bones of children buried in sod,
In graves you'll never see.

HEAVEN'S BRANDING

Janet Parkhurst
Cody, Nebraska - 1995

I dreamed one night I stood before the pearly gates.
Would I know my loved ones there? Some debate.
St. Peter was my guide as we toured this holy place.
I longed to see them all and searched each
peaceful face.

We saw a crew of cowboys roundin' up the
heavenly herd.
One rode out ahead, his horse he gently spurred.
He sat tall in the saddle, I could tell he was
respected.
The cattle corralled quite easily, as calmly
he directed.

My Dad was riding there.

The cattle were quickly sorted; runaway calves
were roped.
I searched the faces for others I knew, it was
as I had hoped.
He stood with others gathered round, the story
that he told
Had brought laughter to each face as his tale did
unfold.

My husband was laughing there.

The branding fire was started, each cowboy took
   his place.
The work was done methodically, it portrayed a
   kind of grace.
From the back of a pickup two little cowpokes were
   takin' it all in.
I heard the deepest laugh from one; I just had
   to grin.

My son was watching there.

Heelers, wrestlers, branders, they all did their job
   with ease.
Work turned to pleasure, that's what it was for these.
A little girl rode up, blonde hair blowin' in the wind.
Sparklin' eyes lit up as though she'd seen a
   long-lost friend.

My daughter was smiling there.

The work was soon completed, to the big ranch
   house they rode.
A feast was waiting there, complete with pie
   a la mode.
A genteel woman rang the bell and hollered
   "come 'n' dine."
She welcomed each one with a smile as they formed
   a dinner line.

My Mom was serving there.

Everyone was seated and bowed their heads to pray,
Thankful for their heavenly surroundings and the
    outcome of the day.
A presence filled the room, peace and love was all
    around.
He stood with hands outstretched; on His head a
    golden crown.

My Lord was waiting there.

GROWING UP
WESTERN

JINGLIN'
THE
HORSES HOME
Janet Moore
Camp Verde, Arizona

There's a place my mind may wander
When the world starts closin' in,
To a time when I was younger
And we neighbored work with friends.

Whenever the day had come to a close
And the work was over and done,
And all the neighbors were headin' back
I'd jingle the horses home.

On a starry night if the moon was bright,
The world was peaceful and still;
I'd gather up the cavvy
And head 'em down the hill.

They'd line out from a work-hard day
And gently plod along,
And the rhythm of their movin' feet
Made a soothin', quiet song;

And the night sounds, soft and peaceful,
Made our spirits fly
As we breathed deep of contentment
Under the starry sky.

Just me and the Lord and them horses
And a night filled with wondrous peace,
Bone weary from a day's hard work,
Yet the wonder did not cease.

Yes . . . there's a place I go in memory
When the world's load is too heavy to bear.
To a place of peace and contentment
That them ponies and I did share.

I think back to that time of my youth
And the job that fell to me,
And even now I have to smile
At that happy memory.

Whenever the world starts closin' in
And my mind begins to roam,
I travel back to my younger years
And jinglin' the horses home.

— RAIN IN —
THE NIGHT
Myrt Wallis
Recluse, Wyoming - 1996

It had rained in the night
Before we rode out.
Our horses' feet
Left perfect hoofprints
Black green
On new grass
Frosted white
By droplets coating
Every blade.
We passed
Wild roses
Made of china,
Golden cactus flowers
Dripping pearls,
And tiny wild plum babies
Dipped in silver.

Dad was up ahead
Single-footing fast.
I was keeping up
By kicking and jigging.
He was whistling
That tune again,
The one that meant
Good grass
Fat cows
Fine day!

There may have been
Other riders . . .
Probably were.
I only remember
Dad and me
And the morning . . .
After it rained in the night.

WILD
MORNING GLORIES
Sharlot Hall
ca. 1924

Once in a wind-swept, sunburned land
Where long, rough hills come crawling down,
44   Crowding the little valley hard
With buttes like paws, rock-clawed and brown,
One great split boulder in the sand
Made spots of shade where wild vines grew,
All hung with swinging bells of bloom—
In sunset colors pink and blue.
Small morning glory vines that clung
Back in rock rifts dim and cool—
And two ranch children all through May
Were tardy every day at school.

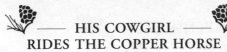

HIS COWGIRL
RIDES THE COPPER HORSE
Linda Hussa
Cedarville, California

Horse heads hung sleepy
over stall doors in the narrow alley
of the barn, she perched on the horseshoe keg,
he leaned on the anvil, while they talked
high school rodeo, decided bits, training,
how to rope calves fast.

Time came she rode away to college,
work, wedding, baby. They talked
on the phone—first tooth and daycare.
Then she bought a horse and rode back home
on the telephone wires.

Three thousand miles apart,
hands in the air, he doubles the colt
or turns it in one swift motion,
then listens.

They talk bits, running martingales,
gooseneck trailers, slick-fork saddles.
Bloodlines. Flying changes.

45

From Linda Hussa, *Blood Sister, I Am to These Fields: New and Selected Poems*
(The Black Rock Press, 2001).

I NEVER WANTED TO "MOTHER UP"
Sally Bates
Yavapai County, Arizona

When you pen the cows and babies
After movin' several miles
Sometimes the two will separate
An' stay that way a while.

The cows commence to bawlin'
And the babies bleat and call
'Til they finally find each other
And they "mother up" 'til fall.

It's like they want to climb inside
That womb they've left behind,
An' the mama seems so worried
That she prob'ly wouldn't mind.

Now, human young'uns act the same—
Just watch a "herd" sometime;
Them little fellers want their moms,
And in their laps they'll climb.

But even as a little "pup"
I never fit the mold,
I didn't want to "mother up"—
Never did it, truth be told.

To "mother up" meant stay indoors
An' study woman's ways,
Bake cookies, sew and curl my hair,
Not see the sun for days!

I didn't want to "mother up,"
How I hated those female wiles.
I cried to follow my hero and dad,
"Cowboy Up!" better suited my ways!

In high school classmates hated me—
At least the ones in skirts —
'Cause I was always hangin' with
Those boys in Levi's shirts.

They talked of cows and horses,
Of ridin' for the brand,
The girls were worried about their nails.
I wanted to make a hand.

I finally learned to fit the mold,
Couldn't stand up to my peers.
The boys all married pretty girls
Who made being wives a career.

I never wanted to "mother up."
Didn't need to be nurtured . . . I thought.
But now my grandkids are lovin' on me
And I'm learning what I always fought.

— THE HIRED MAN —
Jody Strand
Baker, Montana - 1989

My son came home from school one day
and he had a big, black eye.
I asked him how he got it
and this was his reply.

He said, "Mom, some kids made fun of me.
They said dad's just a hired man.
We don't own our own house or cattle,
we don't even own any land.

"They say that we're just drifters,
we can't keep a job for long.
That I'll never amount to nothin'
and we'll just keep movin' on."

I told him, "Son, that's just not true,
those kids don't understand
how many special things it takes
to be a hired man.

"Your daddy's not a drifter,
he'd love to settle down.
To find a better place for us
is why he moves around.

"A nicer house, a higher wage,
a better school for you,
that's why all kinds of people move—
to better their lives, too.

"Your daddy'd love to have a ranch
to call his own someday,
but there was no ranch to hand down,
so he has to work for pay.

"Your dad could go to work in town
and wear a suit and tie,
but that's not who or what he is
and here's the reason why:

"If there were no more hired men,
big ranches would be gone.
One man can't do it all alone,
even working from dusk till dawn.

"Large herds of cattle would be no more.
Just bunches here and there.
The stores piled high with beef today
would someday soon be bare.

"Farmers would have to cut down, too.
Land would just lay idle.
'Breadbasket of the nation'
would no longer be our title.

"Hired man—why, they're just words
but they should be said with pride
for they're agriculture's backbone.
Without them, it would have died.

"And, as to what your future holds,
well, son, that's up to you.
But take a lesson from your dad:
be proud of what you do."

BE YOURSELF
Georgie Sicking
Kaiser, Wyoming

When I was young and foolish
the women said to me,
"Take off those spurs and comb
your hair, if a lady you will be.

"Forget about those cowboy ways.
Come and sit awhile.
We will try to clue you in on women's
ways and wiles.

"Take off that Levi's jumper, put up
those batwing chaps.
Put on a little makeup and we can get a
date for you perhaps.

"Forget about that roping, that will make
callouses on your hands.
And you know it takes soft fingers
if you want to catch a man.

"Do away with that Stetson hat for
it will crush your curls.
And even a homely cowboy wouldn't
date a straight-haired girl."

Now, being young and foolish,
I went my merry way,
And I guess I never wore a dress
until my wedding day.

Now I tell my children,
"No matter what you do,
stand up straight and tall.
Be you and only you.

"For if the Lord had meant us all
to be alike and the same rules to keep,
He would have bonded us all together
just like a flock of sheep.

THE OVERSEER

(in memory of Dad)

Lyn DeNaeyer
Seneca, Nebraska - 1997

Seems a natural fact that spring is mostly wind
    here 'bouts.
Comes howlin' 'round the meadow and scampers
    up the draw
With a sound of heartbroke women, wailin' in
    the night.
Rolls the cloak of winter off the hills an' scrubs
    'em raw,
Tangles with the cries of cranes an' geese in
    northern flight
'Til hands an' critters both start actin' mean an' on
    the outs.

But along the last of May, we're takin' pairs to grass
On a sun-wrapped day, with rose scent ridin' on
    the breeze.
Feelin' good about the calf crop an' all the brandin'
    done;
Remarkin' that the hills is dry, cussin' last week's
    freeze.
Fencin' left to do. A body's got no time for fun.
Lake looks mighty fine for fishin', clear an' smooth
    as glass.

Thunderheads are buildin' so we hurry 'em along.
Two more miles of mesa left before we hit the flat.
Horseback on these ridges ain't a place you care to be
With hell a poppin'. Time to set the steel an' grab
     your hat
'Cause if we can beat it to the meadow, we're home
     free.
I got no clue just now why I'm thinkin' of a song

'Bout angels here among us. I tell the Landlord all
     the same
If he's got a few to spare, just as well to bring 'em on.
The gray mare's duckin' hailstones, runnin' belly on
     the deck
An' when she swaps ends, I nearly grab a hunk of
     gone,
Then pull the leather just in time to save an awful
     wreck,
See the trail where we was headin' lit with jagged
     flame.

But fireworks never linger. The valley's just ahead.   53
Crew's there, all accounted for, and tallyin' the loss.
Losin' stock's a heartache, but it ain't so hard to grin
When you've looked the Reaper in the eye an' won
     the toss.
Somehow, ridin' home I get to pond'rin' on my kin
Whose tears an' sweat are in this ground that buys
     my daily bread.

Faded ink upon the deed that Grandpa signed
    with pride,
Pins an' wires in Daddy's leg; he'd crawled home
    with it broke.
Turnin' out the mare, I brushed the curtain of
    the past
In the scent of Daddy's pipe; Prince Albert's what
    he'd smoke.
Benediction on this day, so I'd understand at last
Which angel dusted off his spurs for one more
    hell-bent ride.

THE — COWTANK

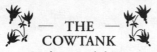

Barbara Bockelman
LaVerne, Oklahoma - 1995

When we thought
No one was around,
We girls sought
The cowtank
By the pens
Near the road
On a summer afternoon.

We made certain
The coast was clear,
Then slipped off our clothes,
Taking one last look
To be sure
No one was near.

Then we'd put our legs
Over the metal rim,
All set for a cooling swim.
There we posed
Grandly unclothed,
Until we slipped
Into the slobbery water
To sit upon
The rough cement bottom.

55

We'd splash around,
Standing up
To let the breeze
Cool every inch and pound.

But the biggest splash of all
Came when we heard this call:
"HELLO THERE, LADIES!
HOW'S THE WATER TODAY?"

Air bubbles rose
As we sank
Into the slimy depths
Of that old cowtank
By the pens,
Near the road,
On a summer afternoon.

INDEPENDENCE

Pat Frolander
Sundance, Wyoming - 1999

Cookie jar empty
Cowboy hat gone
Small boy bootprints lead toward the barn.

Tears on my cheeks
Pain in my heart
Wishing back words that keep us apart.

Down to the pond
I hurry, of course
It's easy to follow the trail of stick horse.

I stop and listen,
Hearing him say,
"I'm leaving this place, I'm going today."

He kicks at a rock
And frightens a frog
Then sits with a sigh on an old rotted log.

He ponders a leaf,
Grabs at a fly,
Captures a hopper, watches it die.

The calf inches closer,
The boy caught surprised
Jumps up and runs, fear in his eyes.

57

I hasten back,
Arriving in time
To greet at the door this cowboy of mine.

I casually ask
Where he has been.
Regaining composure, he says with a grin,

"Feeding your cookies
To ducks on the pond.
Let's make some more, I fed them all gone."

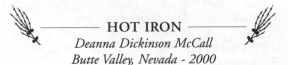

HOT IRON
Deanna Dickinson McCall
Butte Valley, Nevada - 2000

Ropes and wood fire, seemingly total chaos abounds
Amid choking dust and deafening bawls
The call of "HOT IRON" clearly sounds.

I recall Granddad, then my own dad
As they quickly made their way to a calf,
And that old warning call makes me sad.

There's babies and toddlers penned in truck beds.
Three generations gathered to work today,
Yet I recall what the fourth and fifth said.

I hurry back to grab another iron fast.
Only then do I realize the old call
Came from my own lips as it passed.

A COWGIRL
& HER HORSE

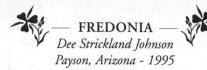

FREDONIA
Dee Strickland Johnson
Payson, Arizona - 1995

I saddle up one afternoon
and happily I hum the tune
of some old plaintive cowboy song.
As if to say I'd got it wrong,
Fredonia shakes her mane and head,
and I believe she's firmly said,
"Cut the horseplay! Let's get on
the timber trail.
Forget the song."

The trail winds upward, twisting, rising
toward the west where, with surprising
artistry, the sun, in leaving,
shafts of light will soon be weaving—
purple, gold and crimson bright—
with empathizing shades of night.
A tremor threads Fredonia's spine
and, somehow, is transferred
to mine.

Among the white-barked aspen trees,
I touch the reins and press my knees
Against her sides. Fredonia halts
and turns to know if she's at fault.
I dismount to lie among
the fallen leaves, once green and young,
now crisp and curling, old and brown;
they cushion me
as I lie down.

Fredonia flicks her tail to say,
"Get up! We must be on the way!"
Refreshing dampness holds me; still,
Fredonia's eyes are on the hill.
Reluctantly, I rise and straddle
the smooth cool leather of my saddle,
then reach to stroke the little mare
who really thinks
we're bound somewhere.

SHE LOVED HER HORSES

Elizabeth Ebert
Lemmon, South Dakota - 1998

She loved her horses. From the time
She learned to walk, she never did
If she could ride there on a horse.
She was a coltish sort of kid
With long slim legs and wind-tossed mane,
No time for ribbons or for curls,
For horses filled her every thought.
She didn't quite fit with other girls
And she judged boys by how they rode.
She never cared for idle chatter,
And if they thought her somewhat strange
To her it did not greatly matter.

And then he rode into her life.
He never noticed she was plain.
He loved the way she sat her horse
And how she held her bridle rein.
The flowers he brought her were embossed
In leather on a saddle skirt,
For jewelry, a silver bit.
He braided her a horsehair quirt,
And slowly, gently, won her heart.
She found him good and kind and true,
And if she still loved horses more
He did not mind. He loved them too.
A son was born who also shared
This love of horses and of leather.
Three hearts in rhythm with the hooves.
Good were those days they rode together.

The truck came hurtling through the night
And took the only things that mattered;
It took her husband and her son
And left her with her legs all shattered.
It took her hopes. It took her dreams.
And left her nothing but her pride.
She viewed the crutch she now must use
And vowed someday again she'd ride.
She never spoke about her loss,
She never spoke about her pain.
And when she cried, she cried alone
And wiped her tears on horse's mane.

And by herself, on gentle mare,
She cinched her old and well-worn saddle
And tried and tried and tried again
Until at last she was a-straddle.
A scabbard for the hated crutch
That must be always at her side.
"My third leg's stirrup," she scornful said.
But now, at least, again she'd ride.
And ride she did through days uncounted
Through sun and wind and storm and fair
All by herself, but not alone,
For memories rode with her there.

63

Then one day out upon the prairie
Her pony slipped and came up lame.
She took his reins, she took her crutch.
They limped along about the same
At snail's pace for some fourteen hours
Before the home place she could see.
Of that ordeal she only said,
"We shared six legs—we each had three."

But from that time, folks came to note
She seldom rode, but drove instead
Out to her horses, where she'd stand
To loving stroke a silken head
That nuzzled for the oats she brought,
To brush the tangles from its mane.
These horses that she loved so well
The only solace in her pain.

They found her empty pickup truck.
They called her name to no avail.
Then up across the stock dam's crest
They followed her three-legged trail.
A mare paced frantic 'round the edge
While in the dam, not struggling much
But still alive, a small black colt,
And, floating near it, was her crutch.

She loved her horses.

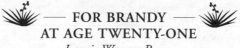

FOR BRANDY
AT AGE TWENTY-ONE
Laurie Wagner Buyer
Fairplay, Colorado - 1999

Over the hill as horses go, but still
coltish, spooked by any movement of
breeze-blown brush or flushed bird,
your red hide shines with excited sweat,
your ears snap and swivel to catch
every errant sound of this soft morning.

High above the world we watch
three black cormorants composing
small circles on the smooth surface
of a seep spring pond, and cars, far
away, crawl along an asphalt ribbon
that wanders where we cannot go.

With knees and heels I pressure your
descent down the steep stony-hided hill
toward the water where the diving ducks,
rising, stretch wide wings and flap
furiously across the lake's face, then
lift like bits of charred ash into the sky.

For one breath-stealing moment, we too
are airborne, leaping into emptiness,
the earth disappearing beneath bunched feet,
your old heart heavy in my tight throat,
my hands grabbing for mane and leather,
until you land stiff-legged on the edge of life.

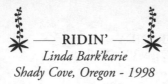

RIDIN'
Linda Bark'karie
Shady Cove, Oregon - 1998

Keep a leg on each side
and your mind in the middle,
sit up straight
and try not to fiddle.
Don't flap your arms
like a big bird in flight.
Anchor your seat
to keep out daylight.
Don't rattle the bridle,
don't jerk north and south,
just flow with your horse
and be kind to his mouth.
When you've mastered all this,
if I may be so blunt,
it always helps
if you're facing the front.

THE MUSTER

"Australie"
(Mrs. Heron)
ca. 1800

Come, mount ye your horses, away let us ride,
For we've many a mile ere the eventide;
The cattle have strayed to the distant plain,
And we must drive them in ere we draw the rein.
So we're off, we're off, we're off,
With the stockwhip in our hand,
And oh, for the fun of a cattle-hunt
With a rollicking bushman band!

Across the gully and over the range,
With a plunge through a creek for a cooling change;
Now over a log or a rock we leap,
O'er hill and on level our pace we keep.
With a gallop, a gallop, a gallop
And a jolly song on our lips,
To the tune of the hoofs and the crashing boughs,
And the ringing crack of the whips.

See the wild young scrubbers come tearing in,
Then away they head, but the tail-mob win;
The horses swerve, and there's many a spill,
But the muster goes on with a shout and a will.
With a yeh, hallo, ya-eh!
And danger full in the face,
And a rageful charge of a snorting bull
But giving zest to the chase.

EL FUEGO
DE SONORA
Virginia Bennett
Winthrop, Washington - 1999

Each night he comes to the ridgetop
Overlooking the rancho below.
Sparks fly from his hooves, dark and flashing,
And lightning reflects in the blaze of his coat.

The hot wind carries his summons
To the mare of the wife of the rancho's patrón.
And, with wild eyes, she paces the fenceline,
As her answers ring off that rocky cañon.

He's on fire, and the Mexican sunset
Gleams in the sweat of his chestnut hide.
And they call him El Fuego de Sonora,
For they know his desires will not be denied.

His sire escaped Pancho Villa
And his dam once served in Zapata's band.
He was born on el Cinco de Mayo.
Never once has he known man's cruel iron brand.

And the mare of the wealthy señora
Has won all the races down fiesta's lanes.
War horses of the conquistadores,
Their blood courses through her hot, royal veins.

She's on fire and the Mexican sunrise
Gleams in the sweat of her golden hide.
And they call her La Luz de Oro,
For they know her desires will not be denied.

On the eve of the summer solstice
El Fuego calls to that palomino mare.
And she flies to obey his every command;
No corral on earth could hold her down there.

Now on cool nights, out in the desert,
He races the wind with the mare at his side,
With blood-soaked flanks, their teeth slashing,
They are out there tonight for the angels to ride.

They're on fire, and the Mexican sunset
Gleams in the sweat of his chestnut hide,
And they call him El Fuego de Sonora,
For they know his desires will not be denied.

AN OWNER'S LAMENT
Veronica Weal
Mount Isa, Queensland, Australia - 1998

So you're going to buy a horse, my friend,
    and fill your life with bliss,
And you picture happy days astride
    when nothing goes amiss.
But those of us who own a horse
    can say, without a doubt,
That the very day your horse moves in,
    your peace of mind moves out.
For firsthand information,
    you won't find a better source,
So listen while I tell you
    what it's like to own a horse.

When you plan to go out riding,
    you will find to your disgust
That your horse has seen you coming
    and has wallowed in the dust.
If by chance it has been raining,
    and he's rolled in mud instead,
You will find that he's changed colour
    from his horseshoes to his head.
When you've wielded brush and curry-comb,
    and polished up his hide,
You are dirty and exhausted,
    and it's far too late to ride.

70

If your horse is going to sicken,
  he will probably go down
With colic on an evening
  when the vet is out of town,
When the mud within his paddock seems
  like half a metre deep,
And you'll nurse him in the darkness,
  thinking longingly of sleep.
After many hours of drama,
  the positions will reverse;
He will probably feel better,
  and you'll certainly feel worse.

If he's going to leave his paddock,
  he is sure to break the fence
On a cold and rainy evening
  when the darkness is intense.
He will clatter down the roadway,
  and you'll leave your cosy fire
While you search around the district
  till you're ready to expire.
When you stagger home next morning,
  having left him to his fate,
He'll be waiting there for breakfast, right
  outside the paddock gate.

When the rodeo approaches,
    that's the time you can be sure
He will cut his leg—not afterwards,
    but on the day before.
You'll call the vet to come and stitch
    the bloody awful mess,
And though you'll miss the maiden 'draft,
    the horse could not care less.
You will watch it from the sidelines,
    feeling miserable all day,
While your horse is smugly resting
    in his stable, eating hay.

If you keep your garden beautiful,
    as many people do,
You will find your horse appreciates it
    just as much as you.
He'll admire your cherished roses
    for their fragrance in the sun
And their flavour on his palate
    when he's eaten every one.
You'll find that many flowers
    have a taste that he'll adore,
And if you grow some veggies,
    well, he'll like those even more.

The price of hay and chaff and oats
 will make you feel quite ill,
And you won't believe the figure
 on the veterinary bill,
But I might as well stop talking,
 I can see you don't believe,
Although you know I'm not the type
 to willingly deceive.
So go ahead and buy him.
 Kiss your carefree life goodbye,
And though I couldn't warn you,
 just remember—I did try!

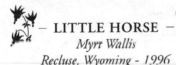

– LITTLE HORSE –
Myrr Wallis
Recluse, Wyoming - 1996

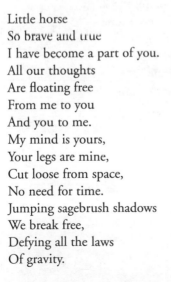

Little horse
So brave and true
I have become a part of you.
All our thoughts
Are floating free
From me to you
And you to me.
My mind is yours,
Your legs are mine,
Cut loose from space,
No need for time.
Jumping sagebrush shadows
We break free,
Defying all the laws
Of gravity.

TO FOXY
Kay Kelley
Alpine, Texas - 1991

Sweet mare, if all I did was watch
As you run and buck and play,
Marvel at your thund'ring power
When you charge and whirl away,
If I just observed your beauty,
Ballerina grace and how
The sun dances on your bay coat
While you're cutting out a cow,

Just watching you gives me pleasure
And I'd feed you just for that.

If all I had was just the feel
Of your warm breath on my cheek,
The touch of your soft, velvet nose
Or your satin hide so sleek,
The companionship we share while
I'm untangling your mane,
The joy of your instant response
To a slight brush of the rein,

If all I had was how you felt,
Well, I'd feed you just for that.

If all I had was what I hear—
The contented munch of hay,
The steady beating of your hooves
As the miles just melt away,
Just to hear your eager nicker
when I catch you for a ride,
Those deep snorts on frosty mornings
As we head for the backside,

If all I had were those sweet sounds,
Oh, I'd feed you just for that.

I've felt your courage in the brush
When a wild one makes her run.
And I know I'm sure a-horseback
When there's cow work to be done.
Yes, Fox, you do so many things
That fill my heart with pride,
Just to know I've got a partner
Wrapped up in your red-gold hide.

Long as I've got one bale of hay
I'll make sure that you stay fat!

THE
— GREATEST SPORT —

Georgie Sicking
Kaiser, Wyoming

An old Nevada mustang
as wild as she could be . . .
I'll tell you all for sure,
She made a gambler out of me.

I forgot I was a mother,
I forgot I was a wife.
I bet it all on the horse I rode;
on him, I bet my life.

The thrill of the chase with my roan
horse trying to give me a throw,
The smells of the dust and the
sagebrush, the rattle of rocks as we go.

Blood running hot with excitement,
mouth getting dry from the same.
In this world, ain't nothin' but the mustang,
roan horse, me and the game.

Mustang is getting winded.
It slows down to a lope.
Roan horse is starting to weaken,
mustang gets caught in my rope.

Roan horse's sides are a-heavin'
and I am all out of breath.
Mustang faces rope a-tremblin';
It would have run to its death.

Sanity returns and I'm lookin'
at the wild horse I just caught.
My prize of the chase,
good-looking or pretty it is not.

A hammer head, crooked leg,
it's awful short on the hip
Little pig eyes, a scrawny U-neck,
and it's really long on the lip.

No, she sure ain't worth much,
for sure she ain't no pearl.
But she took me away from a humdrum life,
right to the edge of the world.

Now, mustanging is a fever like
alcohol, gamblin' and such.
I guess it don't really matter if
what you catch ain't worth that much.

This was before the laws passed that
feed the city people's dreams.
I was lucky to enjoy the greatest sport
of cowboys and of kings.

COUNTRY GIRLS

Marion Fitzgerald
New South Wales, Australia - 2000

Country girls, untamed curls,
Curls embracing the breeze,
Tangling manes in tugging reins,
Frolicking as they please.
Fetlocks thrust, swirling dust,
Saddle beneath their knees;
On spirited mares, they're girls who dare,
Riding with dreams to seize.

Whiffs of bloom, sweet perfume,
Perfumes of leather and foam,
Lathering flaps and bridle straps
And sweating flanks of roans.
Jodhpur seats in saddle grease,
Galloping horses home
On earth's fragrance, unbottled scents,
The country girl's cologne.

Capably tanned, reliable hands,
Hands enticing the best
From frisky colts, in playful revolt,
Steadying them in their quest.
Warming a chill when stirrups hang still,
Stroking away unrest;
The touch of a hand from girls of the land
Strengthen the will of the blest.

Country girls, nature's pearls,
Pearls unpolished and rare,
Untouched by glamour, spurred with stamina,
Groomed with grace and flair.
Harnessing pride on steeds they ride,
The fenceless realm they share;
They're country girls; in all the world,
There's none that can compare.

LISTEN

Debra Coppinger Hill
Chelsea, Oklahoma - 1998

When the horses talk to me,
They tell me many things,
Whats and hows of yesterday,
Why the nighthawk sings.

I learn the meaning of the dance
Between animals and men.
They inspire me to take the chance,
To look back on where I've been.

On this plain where we live,
In the circle at the center,
You receive more than you give,
When privileged to enter.

So I close my eyes in Trust and walk,
And listen to the horses talk.

79

A COWGIRL
& HER WORK

— POST SCRIPT: —
TEXAS WIMMEN
Helen B. Odom
1936

I plumb fergot ter say—
"WIMMEN is WIMMEN," tew,
That allus does ac-com-plish
Whatever thay tries ter do.
Ain't nuthin' never hard
Whin it comes right down ter work;
Why, man, ding bust yore pants—
Thay works harder than a Turk.

Thay'll drop inter th' rear
Uv remudas* carryin' suggins,*
Ter see thet all goes well
With th' waggin' an' its luggins;
Wimmen ain't leather pullers*
Whin atop uv sum caballa,*
Thay kin clim' ter mounten tops
Ter find th' Mex pytilla!*

POET'S FOOTNOTES:

* *remudas*: the saddle horses that furnish fresh mounts;
  when not being ridden, some are used for pack horses.
* *suggins*: cotton stuffed quilts, very lumpy, a part of the
  cowboy's bedding.
* *leather pullers*: those who ride holding on because of
  fear
* *caballo* (ca-va-ya): Spanish for horse
* *pytilla* (pi-ti-ya): Mexican fruit, very delectable; grows
  wild atop mountains, ripe in July.

WHERE
THE PELICAN BUILDS
Mary Hannay Foote
Australian Classic

The horses were ready, the rails were down,
But the riders lingered still—
One had a parting word to say,
And one had his pipe to fill.
Then they mounted, one with a granted prayer,
And one with a grief unguessed;
"We are going," they said as they rode away,
"Where the pelican builds her nest!"

They had told us of pastures wide and green,
To be sought past the sunset's glow;
Of rifts in the ranges by opal lit;
And gold 'neath the river's flow.
And thirst and hunger were banished words
When they spoke of that unknown West;
No drought they dreaded, no flood they feared,
Where the pelican builds her nest!

The creek at the ford was but fetlock deep
When we watched them crossing there;
The rains have replenished it thrice since then,
And thrice has the rock lain bare.
But the waters of hope have flowed and fled,
And never from blue hill's breast
Come back—by the sun and the sands devoured—
Where the pelican builds her nest.

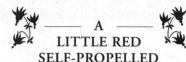

A
LITTLE RED
SELF-PROPELLED
BALER
Lisa Quinlan
San Acacio, Colorado - 1996

Four o'clock summer mornings
When the dew was just right
For making sweet, green hay,
I could hear my dad
Softly wake my brothers
And I wished it was for me, too.
But my legs were not long enough
For the giant orange Case,
And the fat fenders
That hid the tires
Hid me as well.

One hot day at a farm sale
I saw a rusty-colored red
Self-propelled baler.
I climbed up on it
And smiled at my dad
As both my feet
Pressed those pedals perfectly.
"Look, Dad, I can reach!"

I remember being so excited
When we got it home
As my dad greased
And checked it out,
He had to tell me
To sit in the seat
And be still.
"Finally," I thought,
"Part of the crew
With my very own baler."
I knew for sure
I was the luckiest
Eight-year-old girl
Anywhere.

I ran that baler for years,
And I can still remember
The moist mornings
Mixing with the fresh smell
Of that pretty hay.
I would watch for the first
Sliver of the sun
To kiss the world awake.
When the noisy machines
Were silenced for the day,
Meadowlarks
Took their place in song.

Yesterday,
I drove by the Co-op
And noticed some machines
I hadn't seen before.
One of them was a rusty red baler.
I turned around and parked the car.
As I climbed into the seat
And pushed the pedals,
I knew this was mine.
I crossed my arms
On the steering wheel
And rested my chin on my hands.
"Finally," I whispered,
"Part of the crew."

ROUND-UP HAND
Carole Jarvis
Wickenberg, Arizona - 1996

It's still dark at five A.M. in mid-October,
And so cold it makes my toes and fingers ache.
The horses are all saddled and they're ready,
We'll be ridin' after cows by daybreak.

Last night, my husband asked, "You wanna cowboy?
We can use an extra hand if you do."
"You bet!" I answered, figurin' it an honor
Bein' asked to help on round-up with that crew!

I'm teamed with four good cowboys and the cowboss,
And I listen close as he tells us who rides where.
I don't know this country half as well as they do,
And as I tighten up my cinch, I say a prayer—

'Cause I'll never make the Cowgirl Hall of Fame.
My catch rope kinda looks like wet spaghetti.
But I try to keep my horse and me positioned,
So when an old cow makes her move, I'm ready.

And we turn back most of those cantankerous cows,
But every now and then there's one gets by.
Chargin' like a freight train on the downhill,
Her tail up in the air, plumb on the fly!

We're off, old Rose and me, but can't outrun her
'Cause she's got it in her mind she won't be penned.
Straight up the side of some steep rocky hill,
Where badger holes are layin' end to end!

86

With only puffs of dust to mark her passing,
She disappears in seconds from my view.
It's times like this I wish I was a cowboy
So I could show that cow a thing or two!

Seems a cowboy's always mounted on some top horse,
That turns and cuts and runs up hills with ease.
And if by some off chance a cow gets by him,
He'll have her roped and back, slick as you please.

Well, heck, my mare and me, we do our best,
And I know we've shortened up a lot of days.
Took a little pressure off the cowboys,
Even with our unprofessional ways.

And I sure don't mind not bein' called to rope one.
I'm content bringin' pairs out to be tagged,
Or lettin' through the gate the ones they've doctored
(Unless it's that old heavy gate that's sagged!).

Just gettin' out in time to catch a sunrise,
As the first long rays descend across a hill.
Feelin', more than hearin', all the quiet
Accompanyin' the mornin's predawn chill.

Coyotes speak their old coyote language,
Their hunt for food begun before the dawn.
Fair warnin' to the rabbits and the ground squirrels
When they hear the aged old coyote's song.

In fall, the colors changin' day by day,
Greens replaced with yellow, red and gold,
Time to wean the calves off from the cows now;
They're big and strong and almost eight months old.

If you've never been around at weanin' time
When they separate about three hundred pair,
You really can't imagine all the noise
That comes from cattle bawlin' everywhere.

The trucks arrive and haul the calves away,
And still the old cows stand around and bawl.
You have to raise your voice up to a yell
Or there's no way you'll be heard at all.

The day's been long, and Rose and I are weary,
But we held our end up, like the cowboy crew.
And I'll go to sleep tonight rememberin'
When the cowboss smiled at me and said,
    "You'll do!"

HIS PLACE OR MINE
Audrey Hankins
Congress, Arizona - 1987

The owner of this ranch never sees the backside,
He seldom gets as far as the house.
He has things to do and places to go—
Busy making his millions, no doubt.

But I'm grateful to him that I have a job
On this place that I never could buy,
Yet sometimes I feel It's more mine than his,
Just listen and I'll tell you why.

I'm personally acquainted with most of his cows,
Though they don't pretend to know me.
Sometimes my dogs must, "Hold 'em up!"
So the calves and the brands I can see.

The cows on this outfit are numbers on paper
To the boss and his banker, I know.
They don't care which one lost her tail to a coyote
When she was a calf in the snow.

I've been way over on Silver Mountain,
Where the world is all laid on its side,
And you pray no cattle will show up there
'Cause the oak brush is ten feet high.

You're duckin' cedars and snappin' limbs,
And wishin' ol' Roany had chaps.
When a rock rolls loose you don't hear it hit,
You're out of the country by then, perhaps.

I know the hidden canyon off Castle Creek:
It's dry at the mouth but has pools farther up.
When the sun's boilin' down, there's always a drink
For a horse and a man and a pup.

I've been to the homestead down along Oak Creek,
Where two apple trees bravely live on.
Scarred and half-dead, they faithfully bear
Long after their planter has gone.

I know the brushy basin where the big bucks run,
And which pinnacle is an eagle's stronghold.
I've stood and watched the setting sun
Turn green cottonwoods to gold.

And always I've wished I could share with him,
But somehow I fail to get through.
It's like telling someone of a dream you had,
It's not real to him like it was to you.

Somewhere, on paper, this ranch is Tom's,
I know in my mind that is so.
But in my heart and my memories, it belongs to me
In ways he never will know.

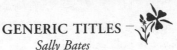

GENERIC TITLES

Sally Bates
Yavapai County, Arizona

I've said it loud and said it long . . .
There's no such thing as a cowgirl.
That name got tacked on Roy Rogers' wife
Fer a cowboy she had too many curls.

A lot has been said about cowboys
Fer as long as they've been around.
Bottom line is . . . that it's a vocation;
The word cowboy's a verb, not a noun.

A female who knows how to cowboy
And can handle herself on the range
Is rarely concerned about gender,
And she never would think it strange

To carry the handle of "cowboy,"
All that means is she's doin' the job.
And she might be a sweet little lady
Or maybe as tough as a cob.

But if you're one who ponders on gender
Or being politically correct,
No wonder you find it confusing
And don't know just what to expect.

Well then, just go on callin' us cowgirls;
It's not a bad word or a "slam,"
But you don't say someone's a truckdriver-ess
Or a carpentress just 'cause she's a ma'am.

91

But if you're gonna call me a cowgirl
To be sure you're politically right,
Then you better start callin' them bullboys
And let's get the gender split right.

 ## COWGIRLS OF THE '30s
June Brander Gilman
Drummond, Montana

We sisters all loved the outdoor life
And were always available for hire
To ride the range in the mountainous terrain
And keep the cattle pushed up higher.
On many a morn when it was feeling its corn
And you saddled your horse for a ride,
You'd darn your luck as it started to buck
Just the moment you got astride.

Then you went flying high like a kite in the sky
And came down like a ton of rock,
But you didn't smile as you hit a rock pile,
And you weren't inclined to talk.
Since no bones were broke, you considered it a joke,
Still, you didn't walk with a skip and a hop;
No, a leg you'd drag as you again mounted that nag,
And this time managed to stay on top.

Your day had begun afore ever the sun
Topped the horizon as a glowing orb,
With the cattle strung out on a mile-long route,
A-graze on the grass and forb.
Many hours you'd spend before reaching the end
Of the trail up the mountainside,
Prodding, yelling and threatening,
And, boy, how hard you did ride
Returning the calves that kept breaking back
And pushing those inclined to lag;
Back and forth and back and forth,
It seemed you were always riding the drag.

But step by step and inch by inch
You would slowly gain the top,
Where you held them still and let them mill
Until all had mothered up.
When your patience grew thin in a situation of no-win,
And you so badly wanted to grouse,
You'd quickly recall the alternative to it all
Was cooking and cleaning the house,
Where the pay was short and the hours long,
Sweating in the kitchen's heat,
And there'd be no praise for the time you'd slave
Preparing bushels of potatoes and meat.

And the cowgirl's life wasn't all work and strife,
There was time to see beautiful things,
Such as lacy clouds, like a heavenly shroud,
That sent spirits soaring aloft on wings.
The sunbeam shining thru the aspen grove,
Creating a dappled shade,
With the white-tailed deer in a graceful glide
Disappearing in a distant glade;
The mother grouse with her brood of chicks
Scratching quietly 'neath a low-hanging fir,
While the Indian paintbrush, a-sway in the breeze,
Kept nodding and bowing to her.

And in late afternoon when you were nearing home
And heard the sound of the babbling stream,
With its promise rash of a refreshing splash,
You'd let loose with an Indian-like scream
And race each other the rest of the way,
Each wanting to be first to dive
Into a pool of water so-o-o cool,
O, yes, it was great to be free and alive!

DRY CAMPS

Sally Bates
Yavapai County, Arizona

It's keen when you camp
Where the water's clear
And the grass is green
'Cause it's grown all year.
There your horse is calm
While the cattle rest
And the cook is kind—
Those camps are the best.

But the trail is full
Of camps that are dry
Where the dust blows hard
And you wanna cry,
Where the cattle bawl
And yer horse won't graze
But wanders around
With a far-off gaze.

For a gal that's raised
Where the water's clean
And the wind blows free
And the grass is green,
Dry camps are the ones
Where the wife can't ride
So she tends the yard
And she stays outside.

In the mornings when sunbeams were dancing,
Then the bay would be ready to race.
I remember him, pulling and prancing,
As I checked him and held him in place.
Let him go, and then nothing could catch him,
He was far too sure-footed to trip.
There was no other horse that could match him,
The big bay with the star and a snip.

But the bay's gallant life is long ended,
And his bones have been bleached by the sun.
Yet, to me, he embodied those splendid
Years of happiness, second to none.
The excitement of mustering cattle,
Pounding hoofs and the crack of the whip!
When I rode like a king into battle
On the bay with the star and a snip.

Now that life that I loved is behind me.
It has gone beyond hope of recall,
Yet those images come to remind me
Of the wonder and thrill of it all.
Then the nursing home where I'm residing
Falls away like a shackle let slip,
And again in my dreams I am riding
On the bay with the star and a snip.

SHOULDN'T WE GO TO
THE HOUSE FOR A HORSE?
Echo Roy
Shoshoni, Wyoming - 1995

When it comes to the two-legged species of man
and the variance in language that we speak,
it's a wonder we ever get anything done
or stay together for longer than a week.

An example that readily comes to mind—
workin' livestock and dealin' with the same—
was doctorin' a sickly yearlin' heifer
we found one spring mornin' in the rain.

Immediately our minds both went to work,
two diff'rent directions with no hope for recourse;
him statin', "You drive and I'll rope 'er right here,"
me askin', "Shouldn't we go to the house for a horse?"

He took that like a slam to the midriff, you know,
masculinity threatened, his impatience foretold
the pace of the day when he charmingly said,
"This'll work if you simply do what you're told."

99

The hairs on the nape of my neck stood up,
which blocked all reason and hearing as well,
so I barely remembered the rest of the plan
as I fired up ol' Blue and circled pell-mell.

"Line 'er out, line 'er out!" he directed from the back,
so I tried, bein' careful not to make a mistake,
but just as he threw, that heifer ducked right,
and seein' he'd missed, I stepped on the brake.

He gathered up quickly in a scary-like calm,
pointin' and indicatin' we'd try it again,
so I drove on real slowly to separate her,
but this was a deal that I couldn't win.

"Can't you go any faster, we don't have all day!"
so I gave it some gas—with no analysis;
but my rearview mirror told the story quite plain
'cause he was standin' in the pasture like this . . .

It was about that time the dog left the scene,
tail tucked as he scattered up over the hill,
and if I had any sense, I'd have followed along,
but now 'twas a matter of will against will.

"Do you think we can do this, time's wastin',
    you know?"
and I thought, "You bet, buddy, just swing yer rope,"
as I once again sorted our girl from the herd
then straightened her out in a nice, easy lope.

And things looked like they'd work, at least from
    my view;
she was headed okay as he made his pitch.
I silently prayed, watchin' action unfold,
when suddenly, abruptly, we crossed a ditch.

Now the language exchanged can't ever be shared
and it's needless to say, we were both some shook up;
but there's no accountin' for stubborn when mad
and as to who was winner at this point—a toss-up.

100

One advantage, the heifer was slowin' down some,
remember she was ailin' and in need of our help,
but despite her tongue waggin', she found
    second wind
just as the next launch crossed over her scalp.

That's when we should have just quit and gone home,
but pride was established and had now reached
    its peak,
and who could'a guessed with those wide open miles
that today'd be the day I'd drive into the creek!

Three hours later, with the heifer still free,
the two of us walked in discordant discourse;
he cussed my drivin', the rope, the rain and the cow,
and by now I was whinin', "If we'd gone
    for a horse . . ."

THE COOK
Myrt Wallis
Recluse, Wyoming - 1995

The boys down on the Boquillas
Were getting kind of lean
The cook was old and greasy
And nearly always mean.

The beef was hardly fit to eat
The beans were always burned
Whenever Cookie called out "GRUB"
A lot of stomachs turned.

The boss was getting worried
Couldn't figure what to do
He'd have to make some sort of change
Or he'd not have a crew.

Then Uncle Mike steps up and says
"I've had all that I can stand
I'll call my niece in Prescott
She's a pretty darned good hand.

"Now I don't know
How awfully good she cooks
But she'll make a welcome change
In the way this wagon looks."

Well, Dorisann was tickled
"I've had enough of town
I'll throw my stuff together
Roll my bed and be right down!"

With her dark and smiling eyes
And her long and glossy hair
She blew into that campground
Like a breath of mountain air.

She cleaned the chuckbox out
And cooked them up a dandy meal
Even though their hearts might break
Their tortured guts would heal.

She filled them up on biscuits
Steak and spuds and chili, too
Lemon pie and chocolate cake
Cornbread, beans and good beef stew.

Until one evening after supper
They were roping a bale of hay
Dorisann, she watched awhile
Then shyly asked to play.

They laughed and raised their eyebrows
But they let her take her turn
She picked up that raggy nylon
And really made it burn.

One by one she matched them all
With plain and fancy whirls
Horn loops and horse catches
Ocean waves and butterfly twirls.

Wasn't long before word got out
About that ropin' cook
Dinner reps came flocking in
To eat and take a look.

Many of them hoped to stay
There were fights to hire on
The boss got tired of the fuss
His patience soon was gone.

He wasn't quite sure what to do
But finally says, "Boys, look
I just won't hire no new hand
Who can't out-rope the cook!"

That thinned them out real fast
'Cause no one likes to lose
Especially to a little girl
In an apron and tennis shoes.

'Til Laughing Jeff rode in one day
His pony stepping high
When told about the outfit's rule
He says, "I guess I'll try."

She matched him on all his throws
Then he matched her on hers
All the while she's watching him
From black hat to silver spurs.

She kind of liked the way he looked
She loved that jaunty grin
The way I heard the story was
She up and let him win!

— HANDS OF LEATHER —
Maggie Mae Sharp
Black Forest, Colorado - 1999

Oh, how I miss those hands of leather
as they last stroked my fevered brow—
I remember strength and love and warmth
Though they're just the sweetest memory now.

Those hands created cords of wood
To keep our family warm,
And they fished for water in the well
on icy mornings on our farm.

Those hands could fashion bits of wood
into toys no one could buy,
Or lance a boil on a killer cow
that no one else would try.

I remember hands of leather
pitching hay from dusk to dawn,
while happy children played
and scattered hay from here and gone.

Those hands drug home a Christmas tree
and set it up before
four excited little faces
peered around the kitchen door.

And I remember how they held my dog,
all limp and close to death—
And how they wiped my tears away
when she drew her last dog breath.

I remember watching leathered hands
hold fast to bridle reins
For hours upon hours
mixed with roan or amber manes.

For weeks on end, they'd crack and bleed
from cold and bitter winds—
But each night us kids were so glad to see
those hands returning, once again.

Yes, I still miss those deeply callused hands
one could mistake for those of any man.
But none played the fiddle quite as gracefully
as my mamma's leathered hands.

LIVING WITH NATURE
& ANIMALS

CATTLE

Berta Hart Nance
ca. 1931

Other states were carved or born.
Texas grew from hide and horn.

Other states are long and wide.
Texas is a shaggy hide.

Dripping blood and crumpled hair,
Some fat giant flung it there.

Laid the head where valleys drain,
Stretched its rump along the plain.

Other soil is full of stones,
Texans plow up cattle bones.

Herds are buried on the trail,
Underneath the powdered shale.

Herds that stiffened like the snow,
Where the icy northers go.

Other states have built their halls
Humming tunes along the walls;

Texans watched the mortar stirred
While they kept the lowing herd.

Stamped on Texan wall and roof
Gleams the sharp and crescent hoof.

High above the hum and stir
Jingle bridle-rein and spur.

Other states were carved or born,
Texas grew from hide and horn.

From Elsa McFarland Turner, *Berta Hart Nance: A Brand of Innocence*
(Austin, Texas: Sunbelt Media Inc. [Nortex Press], 1974).
Used with permission.

MOTHER TO MOTHER
Charlotte Thompson
Battle Mountain, Nevada

She doesn't try to hide her misery;
Her cries echo off of the hill.

It doesn't seem fair, doesn't anyone care?
They act like it's not a big deal.

And they're the first to cuss a poor mother,
but I've raised kids of my own.

And though raising them wasn't easy,
the hardest part's when they all four left home.

She cries and my heart breaks for her,
and she'll cry for a week and a half.

But I can relate to her down by the gate—
My gosh, how she misses her calf.

109

THE RHYME
OF THE PRONGHORNS
Mary Austin
1928

This is the tale that the howlers tell
At the end of the hunting weather,
When the quick rain rills
On the bare, burnt hills,
And they talk in the lair together
Gray coyote and lean gray mate
And little gray cubs that cry
When the wet wind shrills
In the lone, waste hills,
And the rains go roaring by.

Now this is the law the pronghorn makes
For himself and the fawn and the doe,
When the rank wild oats are belly-deep,
And the waning poppies blow.
The young must run at the mother's flank,
But the bucks they run alone
From the time the old year's horns are cast,
Till the new year's horns are grown.

And up they go by the tumbled hills
Where the windy mesas lie,
And the black rock slips from the ruined lips
Of the craters stark and high;
And far they range, and fast they run;
But the howlers mark them go.
Oh, still and fleet are the padding feet,
And many a trick we know!

We bay them down from the feeding-ground,
We fend them back from the pool,
And ever we raise the hunting howl
When the sun-warmed mesas cool.
And well they need both wind and speed
When the gray coyote pack,
By twos and threes from the hidden hills,
Breathes hot on the pronghorn's track.

Oh, the red hawk knows where the gophers run,
The mice hear the elf owl call,
The badger hunts for the squirrel hills,
But man he hunts for us all.
And he has taken the pronghorn doe
And the buck with his gun and his snare;
He has set him a price on the howler's skin,
And tracked us home to the lair.

And now we lurk in the scrub by day,
And now we slink in the dark;
And only the foolish rabbits quake,
And only the squirrels hark.
And we must bark at the mesa moon,
And round by the sheepfolds prowl,
With never a kill that is worth our skill,
To raise at our hunting howl.
And we must eat of the sun-dried meat
Of the herds when the pastures fail,
And we who were lords of the mesa-lands
Must skulk from the white man's trail.

Gray coyote and lean gray mate
And little gray cubs that bark,
Hearing the tale that their fathers tell
Up in the lair in the dark.

— COYOTE SONG —
Linda M. Hasselstrom
Cheyenne, Wyoming - 1999

Looking twice and once again
at shaking grass beside the road,
I see a coyote find her shape
in tawny bronze and black and buff.
She looks both ways before she dares
to run across the highway, dive
beneath the fence and look behind
to see what might be creeping close.
Head up, she turns once more,
sees me sitting on my horse.
She stares so long
I see the dictates of her life
behind her amber eyes.

Then she ducks and leaps—
and vanishes. I'm left to brood.
This coyote learned humility
at birth inside a darkened den.
Now she croons the same
old song each day, repeats the rule
she learned at birth: to live in fear
of us. We call her coward
for her way of staying low.
She shows her skittish pups the tricks
so they'll be safe from humankind.

A coyote will eat anything
that doesn't eat her first: birds
and eggs, fruit and fish, roadkill,
roots and bugs and scraps of trash.
She scorns nothing that will nourish.
The ragged pack may yip together
once the game is down, but each
one slinks away alone at dawn.
In moonlight coyotes sing, distrusting
every bush and stone.

113

So why do coyotes thrive?
We humans trust in heroes,
tell our kids to stand up tall,
to fight for our beliefs.
The coyote slinks and prowls,
escapes if danger shows its face,
then eats and sleeps and runs
with fear beside her. Breathes
in terror every day. And still
she manages to live. Perhaps
she knows a truth we have not guessed.
Perhaps it's only those
who pay attention
who survive.

114

AMONG
UDDER THINGS
Marion Fitzgerald
New South Wales, Australia - 1990

His hairy hands he spat upon
As he prepared to take the grip;
I held my breath and flinched my flank
As he clenched them on my tits.

He squeezed and pulled and stimulated,
Which you think would feel quite nice,
But not on winter frosty morn
When my udder's turned to ice.

Last night, he locked my youngster up
For my mammary glands to work;
They filled so fast, my legs did part,
When I walked, my tits did squirt.

They dangled in the frosty oats
With the temperature down near freezing,
And now that I'm all bailed up
I can hardly stand this squeezing.

To make things worse, young Bradley's come
To stay on the farm with Pop,
And I can see this city kid's just dying
To get his fingers around my lot.

"Come perch yourself on this here stool,"
Says Pop, as proud as punch;
*"We'll make a milking man of you
If it takes till blooming lunch!"*

Now, Bradley's at that tender age
When young boys dream they're men,
Well, he must've been dreaming of Dolly Parton
When he grabbed my teats with all ten!

"Brrrrrrhah!" I bellowed, as his sweaty paws
Pulled and squeezed me tight;
But not a drop fell in that bucket,
'Coz my mammary glands took fright.

Again he squeezed and pulled them
Until they limply hung;
But I knew I had him beat when I innocently released
Some green, warm, slimy dung!

"Strewth, my boots," he bellowed
As he skidded and it splattered;
Then I humped my back and bent my hocks
To release my shell-shocked bladder.

SPLAT! He fell face first and flat,
And cursed Pop from under my udder,
*"Why don't you do what us town folk do
And keep a cow up in your cupboard!"*

Well Pop drop-kicked right up my ribs,
And his language was unrighteous;
*"Get out, you bone-dry lazy cow,
I hope you get mastitis!"*

Once they'd gone, my oestrogen turned on
And my milk flowed thick and fast
Right down through all my quarters
Just waiting for my darling calf.

A gentle sucker, I know he is,
So I urged him to hook on to a teat . . .
But cripes that pain, it's back again;
Last night he grew flaming teeth!

117

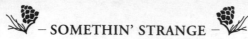

– SOMETHIN' STRANGE –

Jo Casteel
Vale, South Dakota

My kids, half-growed and strappin',
No longer on my knee.
Well, maybe some—at least at times,
'Cuz one were six and one were three.

But Lordy sakes, they came alive
One night—plum scared to death.
They came a-runnin' down the stairs,
Both ones were outta breath.

For somethin' strange had spooked 'em,
Sure as shootin', gave 'em fright.
An awful sound was beatin' loud,
Out there against the night!

But Pa and I were smilin',
For at last our prayers were heard,
But them young-uns' eyes were round and big,
They's in our bed without a word.

"You silly kids, no need to fear,
That noise against the pane,
For tho' you've never heard that sound—
All 'tis is God's good rain!"

118

THE —
GRANNY COW
Audrey Hankins
Congress, Arizona - 1991

We found her on Silver Mountain,
In the oakbrush way up high.
A freckled-faced old granny cow
With murder in her eye.

She shook her bony, toothless head,
Slinging slobber so rank,
And glanced at the dogied hair-ball,
That searched her shrunken flank.

Every year since she was two,
She'd raised a calf for man.
Water and salt was all she asked,
The rest was Nature's plan.

Green grass grew in a field at home,
We decided to haul her there.
She'd raise this last baby in comfort.
She'd earned our tender care.

As we crowded her off the mountain,
Granny charged us time and again.
Lacking the strength to run off,
She suffered the mercy of man.

Granny laid down in the trailer,
Wouldn't get up at the house.
So we, in our wonderful wisdom,
Finally dragged her out.

We laid her upright and slipped away,
Thinking later she would try.
But we'd only hauled her body home,
A faraway look was in her eye.

Her spirit stayed on Silver Mountain.
She even forgot her calf.
After we "saved" the granny cow,
She lived a day and a half.

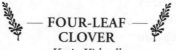

FOUR-LEAF CLOVER
Katie Kidwell
100 Mile House
British Columbia, Canada
1975

I have a little barnyard
where grows the four-leaf clover,
and lucky are the animals
who are the barnyard's mower.

For stomach full of good luck
is worth a couple pounds,
and everyone's a genie
when they rub the magic ground.

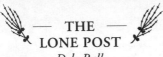

THE LONE POST

Dele Ball
Big Piney, Wyoming - 1991

It might be a gatepost
From a long-ago fence,
Or a telephone pole,
On this pasture immense.

It might be a marker
Of grave, or a trail,
Or an old-timey spring
Where you could dip a pail.

You've all seen a post
On a broad sagebrush flat;
It draws a cow-brute
Like your hide draws a gnat.

Is it company they seek,
Something man has erected?
To care for the herd
So they don't feel neglected?

Or maybe it's a shelter
Alee from the storm,
A buffer of snowflakes
To keep them all warm.

Now you watch when it rains,
The drops fall helter-skelter,
A post's just the right thing
To give top-notch cow shelter.

Say, what of the wind?
That post makes a good break,
It stands staunch and firm,
And protects the beef steak.

At night when the wolfies
Cause them to alarm,
The old cows gather round it
To keep them from harm.

This post, dug and set
With a bar and a spade,
Gives relief from the sun,
Makes a helluva shade!

Why there's hardly a comfort
A lone post can't provide,
It sure don't take much
To keep cows satisfied.

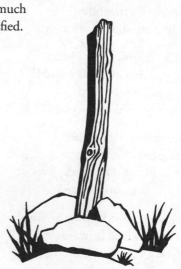

— **STINKY TENANT** —
Terry Henderson
Shawnee, Wyoming - 1995

I lived in a house a hundred years old
on no foundation or blocks,
no crawlway space for plumbing or heat.
It perched on a few gathered rocks.

The wooden siding went down to the ground
where it was beginning to wear.
With chewing and digging, a hole was soon made
by a skunk who decided to share.

More rocks I brought in to cover the hole,
but the skunk just built a new door.
All week I battled to evict my tenant
as the musk odor worked through the floor.

Peeved, I went out and dug a deep trench,
then nailed on some pieces of tin.
That night my kids called as they readied for bed:
"It sounds like that skunk wants back in."

I peeked out the door to look at this skunk,
but it was nowhere in sight.
Wondering where that rascal had gone,
I proceeded out, armed with a light.

It vanished completely into the night air,
nowhere to be seen 'round my house.
"Good riddance," I thought. "I've outsmarted it.
I'm finally rid of the louse."

But as I was gleefully patting my back,
a scratching noise came from the tin.
That skunk was still here, just under the house.
I'd nailed that darn stinker in!

LONE DOG
Irene Rutherford McLeod
ca. 1940

I'm a lean dog, a keen dog, a wild dog, and lone;
I'm a rough dog, a tough dog, hunting on my own;
I'm a bad dog, a mad dog, teasing silly sheep;
I love to sit and bay the moon, to keep fat souls
    from sleep.

124

I'll never be a lap dog, licking dirty feet,
A sleek dog, a meek dog, cringing for my meat,
Not for me the fireside, the well-filled plate,
But shut the door, and sharp stone, and cuff and kick
    and hate.

Not for me the other dogs, running by my side,
Some have run a short while, but none of them
    would bide.
Oh, mine is still the lone trail, the hard trail, the best,
Wide wind, and wild stars, and hunger of the quest!

HANK WARNER'S
LUCKY BURRO

Peggy Godfrey
Moffat, Colorado - 1994

Happened back east in the Mohawk Valley
Hank stopped for a bottle of pop
Heard a fellow complaining about winning a burro
His grousin' dragged on nonstop.

"Five bucks!" Hank offered the griper
'Twas the best deal made that day
Hank loaded the burro in the car he was drivin'
Named him "Lucky" and hauled him away.

Back home Lucky ran with the horses
Kids rode him—he came when they called
Years passed and the children grew older
Lucky was there through it all.

No one knows how the fire got started
When the barn went up in flame
All watched Lucky race from the terror
But none of the horses came.

Men hurried to calm the panic
Horses rearing and thrashing about
None of the horses yielded to men
Not a one could be led out.

In the turmoil of frantic horses
And the valiant tries of men
Lucky returned to the burning barn
And entered the smoky din.

125

Each horse was led to safety
As Lucky showed the way
Though men fought hard to save them
'Twas the burro who saved the day.

Hank Warner's five-buck burro
Who became the family pet
Was lucky and lived to a ripe old age
His story remembered yet.

I think we are one in Nature
All creatures and all men
And we are wise who do not judge
The appearances of friends.

SAMMY BLUE'S
RABBIT CHASING DAYS
Laurie Wagner Buyer
Fairplay, Colorado - 1999

At dusk on a December day his high-pitched yelp
splits the cold silence and the chase is on:
one milk-white blur following the other over the snow.

What a show of speed on the straightaways,
plumes spraying high on the tight twists and turns
into the dark timber where they disappear into a nether-
world of drifts and dreams where surely an aging dog
will finally catch his fast-racing fantasy.

I wait most of an hour in the dimming light,
toeing snow and tamping down my temper.

He returns gimpy, packing a right front paw
and licking up a tongue that hangs nearly to his knees.

He crawls to my side, his eyes saying "sorry,"
knowing full well a scolding's at hand,
but instead I squat down, rest my palm on his head,
aware that tomorrow he won't be able to walk
and suffering the pain will be punishment enough.

SMELL
OF RAIN
Sharlot Hall
ca. 1920

Smell of drought on every side:
Every whirlwind flings aside
Acrid, evil-smelling dust
Like some burning mold or musk.
Wind across the garden brings
Scent of blistered, dying things.
Deep corral dust trampled fine
Stings the lips like bitter wine.
Warping boards ooze drops of pitch
Scented with a memory rich
Of cool forests far away.
In the sunbaked fields the hay
Yields a piteous, panting breath
As it slowly burns to death.
Roses in the ranch-house yard
Turn to mummies dry and hard.
Out of dusk and out of dawn
Every fragrance is withdrawn.
Hot, hot winds, and clear, hot sky
Burn the throat and sear the eye.
Then, at last, a cool dawn wind,
Pitying and deeply kind,
Brings a far-off scent of rain.
Ah, the sick earth lives again!
Herds that straggle dusty-pale
Down the deep-worn water trail

Lift their sunken eyes with hope
To the distant mountain slope.
Lean work horses shy and snort
In an awkward, eager sport;
And the ranch dogs, baying, run
Out to meet the rising sun.
In the yard a woman stands,
Touching with bewildered hands
Wan buds trying to unclose
On a parched and dying rose.

ANOTHER DROUGHT

B. Lynne McCarthy
Buffalo, Missouri - 1993

Fear closes in, running headlong
at my rimrock edge of sanity,
a jaded horse that clatters
across my soul, ribs heaving
beneath a hide lathered white.

"Nothing says it has to rain."

The words fall from a survivor's lips
into the dust of another drought
to scorch and shrivel under
unrelenting rays of Hell.
A weathered hat brim hides
the seventy-year-old brow
creased with reflections
of parched rangeland.

So I reach deep within,
grasping for the strength to face
another drought square on,
scared blind I'll find a dry hole
sucked empty like the pasture well.
The windmill left standing,
still clanking, clanking
over a hollow vacuum.

130

A ceaseless southeast wind moans,
carrying ghostly echoes
of homesteaders who couldn't take
another year, a week, a day
of drought, so they took
a bullet or took out.
This barren zephyr teases
my own hat brim and lets
the sun catch my face.
I began to dig a little deeper
as hoofbeats of my pale horse
rise throbbing in my chest.

THE HEART
OF
A COWGIRL

THE BUCKING BRONCO
Attributed to Belle Starr

My love is a rider, wild horses he breaks
But he promised to quit it and all for my sake.
He ties up one foot and the saddle sets on,
With a swing and a jump he is mounted and gone.

My love has a gun and that gun he can use
But he quit his gun-fighting as well as his booze
He sold him his saddle, his spurs and his rope
And no more cowpunching, and that's what I hope.

The first time I saw him, 'twas early one spring,
A-riding a bronco, a high-headed thing.
He tipped me a wink as he gaily did go
For he wished me to look at his bucking bronco.

The next time I saw him, 'twas late in the fall.
A-swingin' the girls at Tomlinson's hall.
We laughed and we talked as we danced to and fro.
He promised never to ride on another bronco.

He gave me some presents, among them a ring;
The return that I gave him was a far better thing.
'Twas a young maiden's heart, and I'll have you all know
He won it by riding his bucking bronco.

Come, all you young maidens, where e'er you reside
Beware of the puncher who swings the rawhide.
He'll court you and pet you and leave you and go
In the spring up the trail on his bucking bronco.

OUR LAST RIDE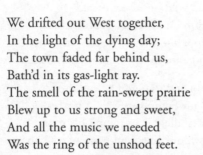
Rhoda Sivell
1912

We drifted out West together,
In the light of the dying day;
The town faded far behind us,
Bath'd in its gas-light ray.
The smell of the rain-swept prairie
Blew up to us strong and sweet,
And all the music we needed
Was the ring of the unshod feet.

We thought of the days that were over,
We thought of days that would be,
We thought of the present in silence,
When you'd say good-bye to me.
I see your face in the shadows,
Just as I did that night,
Though it's years since we drifted together
Out in that fading light.

134

The smell of the silver sagebrush,
The moan of the Western wind
As it blew around our faces,
It all comes back to my mind.
We said good-bye and we parted,
And your trail was new-cut and strange—
Drifting apart to meet no more—
Our last old ride on the range.

Yet I never see a sunset,
But that ride comes back to me.
In the wave of the silver sagebrush
Once more your face I see.
The south wind calls me to you,
So warm, and strong, and sweet,
And your voice is still with me, tender and true,
In the music of unshod feet.

 FOR FRED
Kay Shean
Charleston, Utah - 1997

For some, romance's path is in a look.
And others long to savor soft caresses,
Or search the pages of a Bradford book
To read of heroes bold with flowing tresses.
For some a walk along the beach will do,
While holding hands inhaling salty breezes.
"A loaf of bread, a jug of wine and you,"
Is quoted often as the thing that pleases.
Romance for me will take another bend,
Although I don't reject the former pleasure.
The High Sierras at the summer's end
With cows, and dust and cold beyond all measure.
The most romantic thing I ever do
Is going on the cattle drive with you.

135

— YELLOW SLICKER —
Debra Coppinger Hill
Chelsea, Oklahoma - 1997

She wore his yellow slicker
Though it almost drug the ground,
It seemed to make things easier,
As if he was still around.

He'd left her some big boots
She was gonna have to fill,
But his old yellow slicker,
It seemed to give her the Will.

The Will to keep on going,
The Will to be wise and strong,
The Will to make their dreams come true
And remember where she belonged.

She wore it to feed the cattle,
And when she cleaned the stalls,
She hung it on that high nail by the door,
And remembered he was tall.

She wore it every time
Storm clouds came rushing in,
She even wore it sometimes
Just so the tears would not begin.

She wore it to keep the wet out,
And to hold the cold at bay,
It eased the hardness of the ground
Each time she knelt to pray.

She wore it to chop the tanks,
And when she mended fence,
She wore it on the best of days,
And on ones that made no sense.

She wore it when it was ragged
And had completely lost its charm,
Because, if she was inside of it,
She was back inside his arms.

It's just an old yellow slicker,
But it made her life complete.
It reminded her what's important,
And it kept her on her feet.

She wore it across a lifetime,
And she never felt alone,
She raised their kids, she raised their cows,
And she made their farm a home.

And when she's gone, she tells the kids,
Just hang it on that nail in the barn,
Then look at it, and in your hearts know,
His yellow slicker saved the farm.

RETURN
Linda Hussa
Cedarville, California

After you've gone
I notice your overnight bag
on the bench by the screen door—
shaving kit, freshly ironed shirt.

Anxious to attend the cattle sale,
to sit among other cattlemen
as our calves enter the ring,
and, although there has not been
an angry word between us,
to be away from me for two days.

On the afternoon of your return
I sweep my hair up,
lipstick—Tender Rogue,
the perfume—Il Bacio (the kiss).

138

Chore time comes.
You're not home yet.
I take the ribbon loose,
pull on coat, hat, gloves,

pitch hay to the calves.
The dogs hear your truck coming.
They race to meet you,
barking and wagging their silly tails.

From Linda Hussa, *Blood Sister, I Am to These Fields: New and Selected Poems*
(The Black Rock Press, 2001).

UNFAITHFUL
Jody Strand
Baker, Montana - 1995

The cowboy made a solemn vow
to his lovely bride-to-be:
he promised to be faithful
through all eternity.

He'd keep her only unto him
until death do them part,
and the silly girl believed him
at least, that is, 'til March.

For with the spring, her cowboy changed
his attention seemed to wander,
and suspicion soon confirmed the fact
he was hers alone no longer.

He'd softly tiptoe from their bed
between midnight and dawn,
and often in the morning
she awoke to find him gone.

Lack of sleep soon took its toll,
tempers seemed to flare
and weariness overtook him
when he'd settle in his chair.

Lengthy conversations
no longer did exist,
and she had to stop him at the door
to even get a kiss.

The females he was seein'
were ones she couldn't fight.
There was no way she could compete,
though she tried with all her might.

History repeats itself
and soon she came to know
that for a couple months each spring,
she'd have to let him go.

Because he'd keep his solemn vow
and he would leave her never,
except for those two months in spring,
when he was calving heifers.

140

SKIPPING ROCKS
Marie W. Smith
Somers, Montana - 1988

I rode today across the stony beach,
picked a rounded purple skipper, flat
from constant waters long caressed.

Were you there again? Did you sit
your pony at lake edge, beckon me as I pressed
the stone, then followed its erratic

flight, five giant skips? The best.
Did you smile? My heart played skipping rocks.
You had taught me well, stressed

all the rules. I watched for you at dock's
end. Ah, love, if you could only teach
me yet, how to still the flocks

of longings that rise like gulls, reach
out, ride to me across the stony beach.

141

THE
HIRED MAN'S WIFE
Jody Strand
Baker, Montana - 1989

With the job, your housing's furnished,
    but your house is not your own,
And every time you have to move,
    you grumble and you groan.
'Cause you just got to know the neighbors,
    and your bedroom curtains came.
Your seeds just came up in the garden,
    and now the preacher can call you by name.

You finally got the house fixed up,
    the leaky faucets and busted screens.
You've shampooed the rugs and washed the walls
    and scrubbed and shined and cleaned.
You trimmed the trees and mowed the yard
    and you've got some flowers growin'.
But now that you've made this place your home,
    you'll be leavin' soon, you're knowin'.

'Cause when you get all settled in
    and start plannin' for next year,
You know that he'll sit down one day
    and say, "You better start packin', dear.
I heard about this better job
    where we can run cows of our own.
The pay is good and the housing's furnished.
    So, pack up, and let's get goin'!"

142

You take down all your pictures,
    pack your dishes and your clothes,
Walk through your half-grown garden,
    wipe your tears and blow your nose.
He's trying to make life better,
    trying hard to get ahead,
And he will never understand
    the lonely tears you shed.

'Cause that housing that was furnished
    was like unmolded clay.
You worked and shaped it into your home
    and forgot you couldn't stay.
Now, it's time for you to move again,
    and reluctantly, you'll go.
But part of you will stay behind
    to watch your garden grow.

"How can you start over again and again?"
    some other women ask.
We simply smile because we know
    we're equal to the task.
You see, ranch hands' wives have a special gift
    for accepting what we've been handed.
And to live the cowboy life we love,
    we'll grow anywhere we're planted.

143

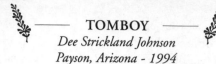

TOMBOY
Dee Strickland Johnson
Payson, Arizona - 1994

I was raised with seven brothers
    near a place called Concho Lake.
There was Jamie, Jeff and Joseph,
    Sam and Seth and Sid and Jake.
So I grew up rough and tumble
    and I made my share of noise.
Romped the dogs and roped the horses—
    I was rowdy as the boys!

Skinny tomboy, seven brothers,
    and assorted brothers' friends
On our little cattle ponies
    raced to hell and back again.
We'd roar down the dry arrora;*
    then we'd all come tearing back,
There was Buzz and Paul and Donnie
    and that rascal Charlie Black.

But one spring, as I grew older,
    Mama firmly told me, "No!"
When the boys went out on roundup,
    Mama said I couldn't go.
Then she tried to teach me cooking,
    how to sew and keep the place;
But my heart was roping yearlings,
    and I longed to barrel race.

144

Andy'd come 'most every evening;
   he was courteous and kind,
And it wasn't any secret
   what that cowboy had in mind.
Every Friday we'd go dancing,
   laughing clear to town and back.
Andy made me feel a lady—
   so I married Charlie Black!

*arroyo

HORSEBACK, THROUGH SNOW
Laurie Wagner Buyer
Fairplay, Colorado - 1999

Horseback, through snow, my great-hearted
husband leads the way the day after Thanksgiving
past ranks of gray-barked aspens armored now
in the afternoon cold, their branches barren,
sap sunk low, harbored in roots that rest unseen,
but certain, while the horses, heaving, sweat
under their heavy winter coats, and I, numb
to the toes, ride lightly as the spirit of spring
that lies buried deep in the earth, my blood
humming like harp strings in a sure wind,
so blessed, so grateful, so aware that someday
our saddles will hang empty in a dusty shed.

146

Once she washed my hair in soap weed;
    while it still hung limp and damp,
She stuck that rusty curling iron
    down the chimney of the lamp.
"Sister," she said, holding up
    a gingham dress she'd sewed,
"Andy's comin'! Now you wear this
    so's your legs won't look so bowed."

Andy was the new young foreman
    of the ranch off to our west,
And of all my brothers' cronies,
    Mama showed she liked him best.
Oh, she was proud that she had made me
    look like something of a girl,
Got me out of faded Levi's,
    forced my stubborn hair to curl.

145

Well, it wasn't long thereafter
    every time that Andy'd call,
And the boys were pitching horseshoes,
    Andy'd linger in the hall.
So he came to be my suitor,
    brought me candy, flowers, and such,
And the night he brought me perfume,
    Well, I didn't mind too much.

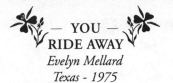

— YOU —
RIDE AWAY
Evelyn Mellard
Texas - 1975

I watched you ride
Away this morning,
Following you
Beyond my sight
With field glasses.
You were sitting straight
In your saddle
And seemed as much
A part of the landscape
As the brown hills
And farther blue mountains.

I lost you once,
And when I found you
Again,
You seemed to materialize—
You and the horse together,
Out of dust and mist
Until you were silhouetted
On the far horizon.

147

From Evelyn Mallard, *In the Circles of Time* (Salado, Texas: Anson Jones Press, 1975). Used with permission.

COWBOY COURTIN' TIME

Elizabeth Ebert
Lemmon, South Dakota - 1997

When Romeo went courtin'
He climbed a balcony,
And some men serenade you
Upon their bended knee.

Leander swam the Hellespont
To reach his lady's side,
But when a cowboy comes a-courtin',
You get a pickup ride.

Sometimes the pickup's even washed
(Will wonders never end?),
But like as not he's brought along
His trusty cowdog friend.

The dog will bark a welcome
(And you know what that means):
There'll be pawprints and dog hair
Upon your new black jeans.

The cowboy'll open up the door
And hold it while you enter.
You know he's gettin' serious
'Cause he sits you in the center.

The cowboy's reeking of cologne—
Half a bottle, you can tell.
You wish he'd shared it with his friend
Who has that doggy smell.

A hairy face on one side
A mustache on the other,
And both of them are squeezin' in
'Til you think you're gonna smother.

You sit there in the middle
Like a rabbit in a hole.
The one is merely droolin'
While the other's droolin' Skoal.

Makes a body sometimes ponder
On the strange queer twists of fate.
Makes you sometimes even wonder
Which one really is your date.

The cowboy'll put his arm around
And hug you 'til you hurt.
And then he starts to pawin'
(The dog, that is) your shirt.

They've got you snuggled there between
Just a pawn within their game.
It doesn't matter where you turn
'Cause they kiss about the same.

Long years have passed since courtin' time
Changed me from Miss to Mrs.
And I'll admit, I've grown to like
Those cowboy-cowdog kisses.

LITTLE DUCK

Carol Oxley
Ashland, Oregon - 1996

When we take vacations from the ranch,
We usually take to the hills;
Packing and camping just for fun
Is the way we look for our thrills.

One summer many years ago,
We managed to finish the haying,
And went to our favorite Little Duck Lake
For two or three days of playing.

We took three horses on our trek,
Two for riding and one packed gear;
We unloaded him and set up camp
Then looked for grazing near.

Way up at the end of the lake
Was a meadow full of good feed;
We turned out the horses to eat their fill,
Content that the grass met their need.

My cowboy pointed out to me
That, should the horses roam,
They had to travel through our camp
And the length of the lake to go home.

Assured that all was in order,
Swimming was next on our list,
And the ritual my cowboy goes through
Is a ceremony not to be missed!

First the Levi's are carefully folded
As a nest for all other clothes,
Then the boots are topped by the Stetson hat
To keep out surprises for toes.

So we left our things on the sandy beach
And went for a leisurely dip.
We were really enjoying the water
When we heard that fateful clop, clip.

The horses were headed for the trail,
My husband leaped forth in his glory,
Donned his hat and his boots and ran round the lake,
But that's only half the story.

Following him in hot pursuit,
I had on only tennis shoes.
If you had come up the trail just then,
You surely would have been amused.

For it isn't often in the wilderness
You come on a scene like that—
Of a naked lady in tennis shoes
Chasing a cowboy in just boots and a hat!

151

LOVE OF THE LAND
& THE LIFESTYLE

THEY KEEP
A-STEALING ON YOU
IN THE NIGHT
Rhoda Sivell
1912

When you think you have forgotten,
And have lived the feelings down,
And have shoved the best that's in you out of sight;
You don't trouble in the daytime,
When you're busy up in town,
But they keep a-stealing on you in the night.

They keep a-stealing on you
When the world has gone to rest,
And bring the past before you bright as day;
You can hear the horses neighing,
You can hear the riders whoop
In the valley by the river far away.

You don't see them in the daytime,
In the city's noise and din;
But when Night hangs her curtain from the sky
They keep a-stealing on you,
Those dear, familiar scenes,
And you know you'll not forget them till you die.

And your old top-horse is standing
With his saddle by the door,
And he whinnies when you're coming into sight;
'Tis years since last you saw him,
You don't think of him in town,
But he keeps a-stealing on you in the night.

And your honey, she is riding
By the river all alone,
And some way it doesn't seem quite right;
For you're hustling, hustling, hustling,
Making money up in town,
But your baby's face it breaks your heart at night.

When you think you have forgotten,
And have lived the feelings down,
And have shoved the best that's in you out of sight,
Just get a horse and saddle,
And drift out from the town,
To the thoughts that steal upon you in the night.

THE
CATTLEMAN'S PRAYER
Jo Becksted
Fort Collins, Colorado - 1952

God, as You know, I am a cattleman
With quite a spread of cows and land.
And tho' I proudly say, "These cows are mine,"
And that "my fence is on that line,"
I realize these things I own,
When all is said, are just a loan.
For I know, God, this great outdoors
And ev'rything therein is yours.

True, I buy or sell for loss or gain
And have learned well the cowman's game.
But, God, when I have gone astray
And You decide that I should pay,
It doesn't take me long to find
How useless are these wares of mine,
And just how small I really am
Here in the vastness of Your plan.

How many times I struggle all night long
To save a cow when something's wrong,
But when I fail, and she has finally died,
You take the cow, I get the hide.
Or when my range is dry and bare
And I stand helpless in despair
Without one thing that I can do,
But pray and wait for help from You.

So, God, in knowing this the way I do,
That all I own belongs to You,
Don't let me get unjustly proud
And think I'm someone in a crowd.
But, help me care for this, Your land,
And all Your cows that wear my brand,
As well as ev'ry horse I ride,
Until I cross Your Great Divide.

155

RIDIN'
Deanna Dickinson McCall
Butte Valley, Nevada - 1999

Have you ever had to bundle up and ride
When it was way too cold to be outside?
It was your pardner who kept you alive
When you wanted to lay in the snow and die.

Have you ever been up high on a mountainside
To have your horse miss a step and begin to slide?
You gave him his head, kicked loose your feet,
Praying you both didn't end up in a heap.

Have you ever been chasing a cow across the plain
Only to go flying before you'd even caught mane?
You went over his head and landed on your back
Thankful the ol' pony's leg didn't snap.

You ride through blazin' sun and choking dust,
Or it's the cold, snow and ice you cuss.
But, through it all, friend, we ride and ride;
156 For us women, it's a matter of cowboy pride.

THE DARKEST HOUR

Carmel Randle
Queensland, Australia - 1996

Another sultry summer's day
   has shuffled to the west
As I slip into a squatter's chair
   to snatch a moment's rest.
On the open east verandah,
   where the moon, just past its prime,
Silhouettes the gidyea
   by the creek and boundary line.

Just two of us, each lost in thought.
   A moon has come and gone.
No rain this time . . . a dry moon!
   Lord, what ARE we doing wrong?
How can two lonely women
   carve a living hereabouts
When all we get are dust storms,
   searing heat, and flamin' drought?

157

Myself—I shared a dream with John.
   This was his family's soil.
For many generations
   it had seen their loving toil!
We'd dream about the future
   as our boys grew into men,
And feel the circle of our lives
   turn over once again.

John taught them basic outback skills
    as soon as they could walk—
They knew of stock and native plants
    as first they learned to talk—
And in between their schooling, well,
    they learned to shoot and drive,
And mend a fence, and fix a pump.
    They'd need THAT to survive!

Then College years . . . how Jack just couldn't
    wait to come back home,
But Jim there found a new life
    very different from his own . . .
A "Guru" all-important . . .
    How I wish he'd keep in touch!
We hope he's happy, safe, and well . . .
    but miss him, oh, so much!

Then Jack came home with Lorna
    as his lovely blushing bride—
Just the sort of friendly girl
    to take things in her stride!
Consoled me when the hand of Death
    smote keenly at John's heart;
Here to give a focus lest
    our dreams should fall apart.

And she gave us Jan, and Little John—
    they're such a bonny pair!
Now snuggled safely in their cots,
    they sleep without a care!
They prob'ly won't remember much
    about their Daddy, Jack,
'Cause no amount of wish or prayer
    can bring my eldest back!

No cure for his Cancer—
    there was nothing we could do!—
And now his lovely Lorna
    is a lonely widow too!
So we sit in friendly silence
    as the moon climbs up the sky
And grapple with the reasons why
    our menfolk had to die.

We wonder where our Jim is . . .
    Will he ever change his mind
And come again to share his life
    with those he left behind?
Why should we bother staying here
    in drought and dust and sand?
Deep in our hearts we know we feel
    this is our Tribal Land!

Sure, I miss the quickened heartbeat
    when my John returned each day,
His smile across the table,
    and the teasing things he'd say.
And the heartache weighs so heavy
    in the middle of the night
When I long to throw my arms around
    my love and hold him tight!

So I sit here, bathed in moonlight,
    and I ponder on the worth
Of striving for a lifetime
    to retain this piece of Earth . . .
Would my forebears rise and haunt me
    if I ever should give in?
Would "to quit and run away" be termed
    "a grievous mortal sin"?

And I think of Jan and Little John—
    perhaps they wouldn't care . . .
They'd find "Home's Where the Heart Is!" True—
    if those they loved were there!
And the years until they're old enough
    stretch grimly out ahead
As they lie there wrapped in silence
    in their comfy baby bed!

Don't treat my cogitations now
      with scorn or faint derision—
When the Agent rings me back
      I must have made the right decision
'Cause he's pressing for an answer,
      and it's me who must decide . . .
Will the City or the Country
      be the future for our Tribe?

The moon has gone. Is that the dawn . . .
      that rosy eastern glow?
A sleepless night with worry fraught,
      but now at least I know!
I'll dial the Agent's number—
      Help me, please, Lord! Guide my hand!
The answer's "No! I cannot . . . will not . . .
      sell my children's land!"

161

LIVIN' FREE
Rhonda Sedgwick Stearns
Newcastle, Wyoming

Just me, a horse, my dog and the wind
Ride to earn our daily fee.
Hard life, perhaps, but we love it, 'cause
We're really living free.

The whole eternal scheme of things
Is too much to understand,
But I'm blessed to live where I can feel
The heartbeat of the land.

The dust and din of man's endeavors,
Thank God, are not too near me—
My chosen work offers special times
To be alone—and free.

Just me, a horse, my dog and the wind,
We've been through much together;
I know they're loyal comrades and friends,
Never mind the weather.

The breeze bears scent of sage and cedar
Where vistas are wide and bold.
Around each bend you glimpse some wildlife,
Just as in days of old.

Mule deer, wild turkey, a bobcat, too—
Bunch of pronghorn antelope;
Coyote, meadowlark, prairie sage grouse,
Jackrabbit on the slope.

And me, this horse, my dog and the wind
Know we're each part of the whole,
As all we see and hear and smell
Exists in our own soul.

Horizons reach infinity,
Or some such faraway place.
We recognize buttes, creeks and canyons
Like lines in some friend's face.

Beneath all this there pounds in our ears
(Like a drummer in a band),
The mighty, unchanging sound we love—
The heartbeat of the land.

Just me, a horse, my dog and the wind
Ride on to our destiny.
Please don't suppose we fail to cherish
This gift of living free.

THE FIRST SURE SIGNS OF SPRING
Carole Jarvis
Wickenburg, Arizona - 1997

Out where the open prairie spreads wide
and the wind makes sagebrush sing,
The snow has pulled back to the hills.
It's the first sure sign of spring.

There was extra hair in the currycomb
when I saddled my horse at dawn,
And along the creek behind the barn,
the ice is finally gone.

As the morning sky turned a pastel tint,
I heard a familiar old call.
Canadian geese passed right overhead,
the first ones I've seen since last fall.

The old mama cat just had kittens,
and the ewes are about to lamb.
Our milk cow, Grace, had her calf last week,
the kids named him Abraham.

As the buds swell on the willow trees,
and I spot the first springtime flower,
I'm aware these are indicators:
winter is relinquishing power.

Which is fine, I'm tired of shoveling snow,
and I'm glad for more daylight hours.
They help cut down on the loads of wood
our faithful old stove devours.

But even without all the other signs,
I'd know spring has arrived once more
By the pile of mud-covered overshoes
we put on and take off at the door!

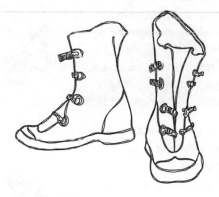

165

AN
OLD MONARCH
Barney Nelson
Alpine, Texas - ca. 1988

I'd unsaddled my ol' pony
    and turned him out to graze.
He'd given me some trouble,
    hadn't rode him in several days.
And sometimes when my horse is fresh,
    now that I'm gettin' older,
I get to wondering if it's time
    to quit, 'fore I get any colder.

Then past my eyes, on tremblin' wing,
    drifts a monarch butterfly.
Once a worm, now paper wings
    take her halting through the sky.
More fragile than the thinnest glass,
    those wings of orange and black,
Yet once a year she makes a trip
    from Canada to Mexico and back.

Through storms and winds and birds of prey
    and some collector's net,
A trip not possible for a butterfly,
    but they ain't convinced her yet.

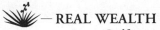 — **REAL WEALTH** —
Peggy Godfrey
Moffat, Colorado - 1992

My neighbors don't live close to me
But we've each got our niche
Government says this area's poor
Our secret is: we're rich.

My wealth won't buy insurance
It won't trade in for much
But "rich" to me is measured
By things no one can touch.

The hint of mint in native hay
Fresh, sweet mountain air
Owls perched high in cottonwoods
A golden eagle pair.

Sheep that run toward my voice
Love in a little boy's eyes
The frying smell of just-caught trout
A winter when nobody dies.

The pleasure of making a garden
Soft soothing drizzles of rain
One dazzling double rainbow
Good lessons that come without pain.

Summers that age into autumns of gold
Wind humming songs like a choir
Sun shining bright on crystals of ice
That glitter like diamonds on fire.

Courage to face disasters
Laughter to lighten the load
Humor to flavor the tasteless times
Common sense to level the road.

Joy filters through my senses
I know this life is healthy
Won't build up my bank account
But damn sure makes me wealthy.

SURE AM LUCKY

Jo Casteel
Vale, South Dakota

Labor Day is over
And the day was darn sure fun,
We jawed some with our neighbors,
And danced when day was done.

We tipped a few in honor
Of the summer's work gone by,
But my belly flipped like flapjacks,
So I stopped to wonder why.

I guess the reason's simple,
And as clear as clear can be.
Dang near everybody
Goes back to work, ya see.

For young'uns, back to school,
And behind a desk for some.
But for me, it's open prairie
To get some fencin' done.

Now, I figure I'm sure lucky—
No slave to clock or bell,
And I'm breathin' all God's beauty—
There ain't nothin' I must sell.

So often I've forgotten,
To say "Thank You" to the Boss
For givin' me the work I love—
For givin' me a hoss.

100 YEARS FROM NOW
Doris Daley
Calgary, Alberta, Canada

100 years from now,
   if the world's still in the game,
May the earth recall our footprints,
   may the wind sing out our names.
May someone turn a page and hearken
   back upon this time,
May someone sing a cowboy tune
   and someone spin a rhyme.

History buffs will study us
   and time will tell its tales
Our lives will be a brittle pile
   of cold and quaint details.
A scrap of faded photograph,
   a news headline or two . . .

But life was so much more, my friend,
   when the century was new.
100 years from now,
   don't look back and think me quaint,
Don't judge and call me sinner,
   don't judge and call me saint.
We lived beneath the arch
   with a mix of grit and grace,
Just ordinary folk in an
   extraordinary place.

170

So 100 years from now
   hear our ancient voices call,
Know that life was good
   and the cowboy still rode tall.
Wildflowers filled our valleys
   and the coyotes were our choir.
We knew some wild places that
   had never known the wire.

We raised stout-hearted horses,
   we'd ride and let 'er rip
We sweated 'neath the summer sun
   and cursed at winter's grip.
We took a little courage
   when the crocus bloomed in spring.
We loved beneath the stars
   and we heard the night wind sing.

We buried and we married,
   we danced and laughed and cried,
And there were times we failed,
   but let the records show we tried.
And sure, I have regrets;
   I made more than one mistake
If I had it to do over,
   there are trails I wouldn't take.

But the sun rose up each day,
   we'd make it through another year.
We'd watch the skies and count our calves
   and hoist a cup of cheer.
We knew drought and fire and heartache,
   we knew fat and we knew bone,
But we were silver-lining people
   and we never rode alone.

So, friend, if you are reading this
   100 years from now
Understand that we were pilgrims
   who just made it through somehow.
We've crossed the river home and
   we left but one request:
100 years from now,
   think back kindly on the West

And ordinary folk,
   no special fate, no special claims,
But 100 years from now,
   may the wind sing out our names.
Know the times were good
   and we rode the best we know.
We loved the West, we kept the faith,
   100 years ago.

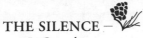

– THE SILENCE –
Jo Casteel
Vale, South Dakota

I stopped atop a hill
Just for a moment, Pake and me,
And heard the muted silence
Of the land that sets me free.

And for that precious moment,
A sound could not be heard.
My horse stood very silent
And so did each and every bird.

The wind, it didn't whistle.
There was no rustlin' of the sage.
The land was ghostly quiet,
Like the comin' of one's age.

And for a gracious moment,
I pondered bein' blessed.
How many folks have never heard,
I never could have guessed.

But I 'magine there are millions
Who have never heard the sound
Of a place immersed in quiet,
With God's splendor all around.

And I s'pose that I feel sorry
For them who've never heard
The gentle, awesome quiet
That surrounds the Master's Word.

— WRONG —
ROAD

Audrey Hankins
Congress, Arizona - 1991

Fed up with owners
Wearing out a dream
In the short span
Of four or five years,

They jointly agreed
To quit the ranches
For house of their own,
The edge of town.

No more
Painting shabby kitchens
Planting flowers, trees
Moving before they bloom.

Her cowboy
on screeching steel monster
Digs
for a living
in dirt.
Cowdog toenails grow long,
Cowponies doze in the sun.

Why does she hear
the jingle of spur
Hoofbeats, whinnies, and calls?

Her spirit lies chained
Afraid life will end
While she still dreams
Of living again.

174

OBSERVATIONS
ON
LIFE & MEN

— MAN-SIZED —
JOB
Sharlot Hall
1924

"Wimmin's bizness, it's to cook,
Keep th' house a-goin',
See th' pigs an' chickens fed,
Do a little hoein'
In th' garden summer times,
Jist to keep things growin'!
Cowmen don't like garden dirt
On their han's an' faces.
You won't find no garden truck
'Round real cowmen's places.
That's a job fer wimmin folks,
Like milkin', churnin' butter.
Cowmen never milks no cows.
Hain't no time ter putter.
Keeps me humpin' ridin' range,
Brandin', ropin', tyin';

Runnin' the whole outfit right—
Wimmins got no use tryin'.
Couldn't run this ranch like me—
Sure, ye couldn't, Maw.
This job calls fer intellec' . . ."
(Chaw—spit—chaw).

TWO DOGS
Deb Carpenter
Rushville, Nebraska

A pot of coffee sat between them
at The Cuny Table Cafe.
'Tween bites of blueberry pie,
they talked of the sun and the rain.

They talked of the moon and the stars.
They talked of stillness and breath.
They talked of good and evil.
They talked of life and of death.

"I have two dogs inside me,"
spoke the elderly medicine man.
My father, a rancher, sat and listened
to the primal story at hand.

"One dog is dark, the other is light.
They growl and they show their teeth.
They will fight to the death over my soul.
The winner takes all, you see."

177

"Which one is stronger?" asked my father.
"Which dog will win the prize?
The light or the dark, the good or the evil?
Where's the heart go when it dies?"

The medicine man tipped up his cup,
ate another bite of his pie.
"Both dogs are strong, and the fight will go on
for the last remains of my life.

"I never asked why they exist
or why I'm called to be their host.
But I hold the key to the dog who wins,
it's the one I feed the most."

Publishing history: *Yuowanca*, 1998; *Nebraska Life Magazine*, Jan/Feb 2000

HATS OFF
Charlotte Thompson
Battle Mountain, Nevada

You know I've been around awhile,
you might say I've paid my dues.
I've known cowboys and punchers,
waddies and twisters,
and quite a few good buckaroos.

And you know they have each one been different,
but they are also all just alike.
I can tell you of one single thing
that makes everyone want to fight.

It's something that seems pretty simple,
but I've seen this happen more than just once.
And if you've ever done it, when I tell you this
you're going to feel just like a dunce.

A cowboy's hat is part of his clothing,
and he don't care what it looks like on you!
If he hung his underwear up there by the door,
would you have to try them on for size, too?

178

— MORTGAGE —
ONE GOOD WIFE
Yvonne Hollenbeck
Clearfield, South Dakota - 1999

When the banker pays a visit
to check your inventory,
the way he values assets, folks,
is quite a different story

than the values placed upon them
by the one who sells insurance;
and if them two would switch their jobs,
it would really make a difference.

The first thing that the banker does
is try to claim your land;
he says it's really not worth much
but on the other hand,
he needs it for security
with the cattle market down;
but he can't loan you cash on it
'cause it is only ground.

The value of your cattle
is the price the packer pays;
your machinery—it's not worth a dime,
it's seen its better days.

You can't borrow on a good old horse,
you can't borrow on your wife;
your house ain't worth a tinker's damn
and neither is your life.

But here comes your insurance man!
He sings a different song,
and says that horse is worth a lot!
You knew that all along.

He says you need a policy
just in case it meets its fate;
and you'd better have a BIG one
on your kind and loving mate.

He says she's worth a million
if you figured up the cost
of hiring folks to do her work;
why, she'd really be a loss!

What about those buildings
that the banker said was junk?
If disaster took just one of them,
you really would be sunk!

And if lightning hit some cattle,
the loss would be immense;
you've got a hundred thousand
in just windmills, tanks and fence.

When that agent finished tallying,
it looked like we were wealthy;
the way he figured assets
made our finances quite healthy.

So, I hope you get my point
in them two switchin' jobs, you see,
'cause if bankers sold insurance,
not very much you'd need.

180

And if insurance agents
made the agriculture loans,
we'd all be driving brand new cars
and living in new homes.

We'd be looking pretty prosperous,
and live a *"rich man's life,"*
instead of buying life insurance,
you'd just mortgage One Good Wife!

181

VERA

Carmel Randle
Queensland, Australia - 1995

In a lonely outback homestead
Quite remote from city life
Lay the station-owner dying—
By his side, his loving wife.

And he tried to speak a little,
So she bent her head to hear—
"Remember when I met you, Vera?"
"Yes, I remember, dear!"

"I didn't have a penny, but
You loved me just the same,
And one fateful winter's evening
You agreed to take my name."

"Yes, dear! I remember that!"
His loving wife agreed.
"Then you came out here, and worked so hard
To fill my every need.

Depression brought us hard times—
But you stood here by my side
Through the drought of nineteen-thirty-two
When all our cattle died.

But, Vera, you were always there!"
She quietly said, "That's right!"
"And even when I went to war—
You didn't want to fight

But you joined the nursing service
And were always near at hand
To lend support!" She quietly spoke,
"I'm glad you understand."

"Then back here on the property
We reared our only child,
But we lost him, Vera—lost him!"
"Yes, I know," she sadly smiled.

"Now the bank is taking over
And there's one thing that I grieve—
I've worked so hard so many years
But I've nothing much to leave!"

"Don't worry now, my darling,
Some dreams do come unstuck!"
"You know what, Vera?" "Yes, Darling?"
"I think you're bloody bad luck!"

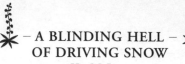

– A BLINDING HELL –
OF DRIVING SNOW
Kit McLean
Winthrop, Washington

A blinding hell of driving snow
The pitch of a hill too steep
Down the ledges of rocks and ice
The coulee's drifted deep

Behind the bunch of gaunted cows
Dark shadows in fading light
Shove them toward the home corral
Each step a bitter fight

Played-out broncs on trembling legs
The norther blows down the draw
The hat pulled down, a face tucked in
Each hand a frozen claw

Into the fast-approaching night
The agony goes on
Each step a small eternity
The will is nearly gone

At last the long-awaited gate
Soon hay piles tossed around
Saddles pulled from weary backs
"Coffee's on!" a welcome sound

Shadows cling to the cabin wall
Outside the wind blows cold
Huddled 'round the old black stove
A modest story's told

184

The glint of light from a sunken eye
Faces drawn and gray
Tell the truth more than the words
The price they had to pay

JULY
THUNDERSTORMS
June Brander Gilman
Drummond, Montana

The distant hills were under a shroud,
A blackened haze from a thundercloud
Released a torrent of silver drops
That peppered the earth like fired buckshot.

The nervous fillies, with tails a-kite,
Raced down the road in sudden fright
Of the lightning bolts and thunderous sound;
Their hoofbeats receding as they galloped on.

185

The cattle all bunched with backs to the storm,
Creating a picture of artistic form.
Branches broke off from the trees a-blow,
And loose tarps blanketed the east fence row.

The rancher sat, just gazing out,
Happy and sad—turnabout.
The country was dry and needed rain,
But its timing was really off again.

For out in the field was a depressing scene,
Winding windrows of grass, once green,
Were rapidly turning to blackened hay
From the sudden rainfalls, day after day.

The hired hand came sauntering in,
And on his face was a big, wide grin.
Seating himself, with arms on chest,
He happily remarked, "More rain, more rest."

The rancher swiveled in his hard-backed chair
And fixed the culprit with an icy stare.
"What'd you say; I didn't catch the last?"
The ranch hand replied, "More rain, more grass!"

— **GEEZERS AND CRONES** —
Gwen Petersen
Big Timber, Montana - 1995

Two old cowpokes, Jake and Jerome,
Hung up their saddles and went to the Home,
For Old Man Time has burned his brand
On these elderly cowboys once so grand.
Now they sit in hallways, leanin' on canes,
Talkin' 'bout history and old campaigns,
Talkin' 'bout horses they've rode on the range,
Talkin' 'bout old days and the way things change.
And sittin' across from the ancient old men,
Are two old cowgirls a-wonderin' just when
Them decrepit old coots will quit reminiscing,
And start talkin' 'bout some old-fashioned kissing.
Now Agnes and Alice, once pretty cheeky,
Worry most now 'bout bladders bein' leaky.
"Ya know," said Agnes, "it's purty durn borin'
Just watchin' them geezers 'n hearin' 'em snorin'.
What do ya say we liven things up,
Get undressed and strut our stuff."
"Good idea," Alice replied,
"Betcha them boys'll go plumb wild-eyed."
Well, the gals got nekkid and pushin' their walkers,
Went truckin' down the hall like old crone stalkers.

187

It took 'em awhile and quite a few pains
To catch them geezers, leanin' on their canes.
The old girls jiggled like Goodyear rubber,
Parts of 'em wiggled like tapioca blubber.
They promenaded on with a git-a-long hitch,
Tryin' not to scratch where anything itched.
Upon this sight, the old fellers gazed,
Then looked at each other, plumb amazed.
"What the hell's that?" Jake asked, frowning.
Said Jerome, "I dunno. But it sure needs ironing!"

KEEPING AN EYE OUT

(for Hudson, who cowboyed for the Diamond A
before going to work at the sale ring)

Linda M. Hasselstrom
Cheyenne, Wyoming - 1998

The way we use ta break *HAWK!*
ropin' horses was *PATOOEY!*
if you wasn't too choosy
about the horse, *HAWK!*
to saddle him up, git on, an *PATOOEY!*
rope a steer.
About a thousand-pound steer.
Tie the rope on the saddle horn *HAWK!*
an' then jump off. *SQUIRT!*

The horse'd go one way
and the steer another.
Jerk that horse flat on his side. *HAWK!*
About the second or third time *PATOOEY!*
that horse got his feet
jerked out from under him
he started watchin' the steer
the way he oughta. Yep. *HAWK!*
When ya started workin' a horse
after that, he knew enough
to keep an eye out. *PATOOEY!*

Pete Lemley, when he rode those
green broke horses,   *HAWK!*
he always carried a .45 strapped on his hip.
He didn't kill rattlesnakes
or coyotes.   *SUCKUGGH—*
Said he liked 'em cause they kinda   *PATOOEY!*
thinned out the hunters
that didn't keep an eye out.
Nope. Pete said he carried the .45
for one reason: the damn horse
might throw him an break his leg
down in the Badlands
and then run off.   *SPIT!*
He said he'd probably try crawlin' home,
but after two or three days
without water in the middle o' July,
he might decide it was his own fault
for not keepin' an eye out,
and he didn't wanta suffer any more.   *PATOOEY!*